HOW TO GET
MARRIED...
$\mathscr{A}$GAIN

HOW TO GET MARRIED...

A GUIDE TO SECOND WEDDINGS

JILL CURTIS

Hodder & Stoughton
LONDON SYDNEY AUCKLAND

First published in Great Britain in 2003

10 9 8 7 6 5 4 3 2 1

British Library Cataloguing in Publication Data
A record for this book is available from the British Library

ISBN 0 340 86127 4

Printed and bound in Great Britain by
Bookmarque Ltd, Croydon, Surrey

Hodder & Stoughton
A Division of Hodder Headline Ltd
338 Euston Road
London NW1 3BH
www.madaboutbooks.com

This book is dedicated to
every bride and groom seeking happiness
a second time around.

'Few of us love others for what they really are. Most of us love what they imagine in others; they love their own idea in somebody else.'

GOETHE

Contents

Part Two: Wedding Bells Are Heard Again

Acknowledgments

In Britain at the start of the twenty-first century an ever increasing percentage of all marriages are *second* marriages; the figure is rapidly approaching the statistic for the US which is 50 per cent. It was therefore all too easy to find and talk to second wives and second husbands and also to men and women who were marrying for the first time but whose spouses had been married before. I also had little difficulty in seeking out those who at the time we met were *third* husbands or *third* wives. I say 'at the time we met' because by the time I checked what I had quoted with one husband he was embarking on his fourth wedding!

So many of these men and women generously gave their time to tell me about their experiences of planning a *second* wedding that they are too numerous to name here. They shared with me their memories of the build up to their special day, and together we laughed about some of the things which happened, and there were tears too about the unexpected complications which cast a shadow over a day which should be trouble-free and memorable. My thanks to all of them, for without their help it would not have been possible to write this book.

Introduction

This book is for the ever growing number of men and women who find themselves about to embark on a *second* wedding – a wedding where one or both of the bridal couple have been married before. Every wedding involves many more people than the two who are about to make their promises and there is an endless list of things to get sorted, but when it is a second wedding the people and problems can multiply beyond measure!

The most visited pages on my website, www.familyon wards.com, are those about marriage and especially those that deal with second weddings. I get a host of e-mails from brides-to-be, second-time grooms, past and future mothers-in-law, future step-parents, children who will be witnessing the remarriage of a parent, and even from friends who are confused about some aspect of a second marriage. Sometimes the questions come from a first-time bride or groom marrying someone who has been married before, or they may arise when both parties have been married previously and want advice on celebrating their second wedding. Without exception, the questions fall into three categories: 'Please tell me if there is any proper etiquette for second weddings', 'How can I make this wedding really special?' and, perhaps the most poignant, 'I don't want to hurt anyone but already I seem to be upsetting a lot of people.'

So why is planning and organising a second wedding so different? A second wedding brings with it a host of new situations and areas of possible conflict. For the first-time bride or groom there may be hiccups during the planning of the wedding, but there are already numerous books and bridal magazines available to help with the smooth running of the wedding day. There are endless lists of how many pots and pans you will need to set up home and advice about how to look beautiful at your engagement party. I have assumed that this is not what you want, but, rather, a guiding hand to help with the multitude of difficulties and decisions that arise in planning a second wedding.

Anyone who is remarrying has the experience of their first marriage behind them, usually with vivid memories of the first wedding day itself. You will soon find out how many ghosts from the past need to be laid to rest before you can approach your second wedding in the way it should be celebrated, with joy and happiness. There will be people close to your first partner who will be affected by the marriage and great confusion can be caused when relatives, people connected with your ex, and even friends have their say, which undoubtedly they will do.

> The largest proportion of all marriages in the UK today are *second* marriages for one or both partners.

Today, with the increase in the divorce rate, more and more people are getting married for a second time, although a second marriage can also come after the death of a much loved spouse. It can be very painful and frustrating for a couple who are head-over-heels in love and want to marry to be confronted by unexpected problems and decisions which were not there to trouble a first-time bride or groom.

As so many second weddings are those of a man or woman who already has children from an earlier relationship, a great deal of care needs to be taken over where the children fit into the picture. I have therefore placed special emphasis on how you should tell the children about your forthcoming wedding, and also about the different roles the children can play on the wedding day itself. A warning about the difficulties encountered by second families comes from one stepfamily organisation: 'Despite initial love and commitment, stepfamily *stress* eventually overwhelms well over half of the couples who remarry.' Although this refers to families in the United States, statistics confirm it to be the same in other countries as well. So beware, and tread carefully.

Many a bride glows with the thought that this second time she can plan her wedding day in just the way *she* wants to. Confidence comes with maturity, and with the experience of one wedding – and relationship – behind her, the bride will know what she does *not* want this time around. And for a second wedding, the chances are the couple will be paying for it themselves, and be less dependent upon a parent who is picking up the bill.

I hope this book will provide answers to those three main questions: 'Yes, there are rules of etiquette to be considered in connection with second weddings, and they all help to make the day run on well-oiled wheels.' 'Yes, there are many ways to make your wedding special.' And, thirdly, 'With a careful and considerate eye on the people around you – and this includes you and your new love – there should be no need for tears on the special day because something or someone was not thought about.'

Many people expect their wedding day to be one of the best days of their lives. There is no reason why this should not be as true of second as of first weddings, so read on.

JILL CURTIS
LONDON 2003

PART ONE:

Putting the Past
Behind You

♥

A second chance

> 'A lady's imagination is very rapid; it jumps from admiration to love, from love to matrimony in a moment.'
>
> JANE AUSTEN, *Pride and Prejudice*

Learning to trust someone new

'Never again' is what a man or a woman with a broken heart often proclaims. And yet, as time goes on, there is that urge once more to find that special person with whom to share one's life. You may have discovered that it was not so easy to get into the dating game again. And now that you have dared to put your toe in the water once more you may be filled with happiness to have found someone. You have discovered that special someone you can trust and love, and who loves you back.

Don't be anxious if somewhere at the back of your mind you remember having read the statistics which show a higher number of second marriages break up compared to first ones. This time you know you will be more prepared for what marriage actually *means* and you will have maturity on your side. Be kind to yourself and your partner, and seize this second chance of happiness.

> Marriage is back in fashion: in the year 2000 the number of couples getting married in the UK rose for the first time in eight years. One of the reasons for this increase was the large rise in the number of *second* unions.

It is important that you and your husband- or wife-to-be accept that feelings associated with an earlier relationship must be truly understood and resolved, so you are not likely to make the same mistake again. At first, after your divorce, you may have doubted your ability to choose a new partner; and when you met your intended you found that you were caught in a push-me-pull-you situation: wanting a close and intimate relationship very much indeed, but at the same time being fearful of making another mistake. Hopefully you will have talked through these doubts, so that they are now behind you both and you are no longer wary about setting out in the matrimonial boat again.

Keep in mind, too, that if you have been married before, you should understand more about what makes a relationship work, and how you have to be on the look-out for danger signals. You will know that nothing should be taken for granted. Unreal expectations and assumptions should be a thing of the past, and you will be more aware of your own psychological make-up and what makes you tick. This time you will be prepared for that period, once the wedding-day euphoria has died down, when you get on with everyday married life. You will know that when the immediate excitement evaporates a little, it is not a sign that your marriage is failing, but of reality setting in. You won't collapse – and neither will your marriage – at the first disagreement you have with your new love.

Here are extracts from e-mails I received from three people who have seen what went wrong before, and who now have an optimistic approach to the future:

Pamela: 'I loved being married, and when my first marriage broke up I took a long time to recover. I made sure I was well and truly over Bob before I began to look around. Even so, I was cautious, but Don's lovely personality and integrity helped me to trust again. We are marrying in May. Is it OK to splurge out and have a proper wedding?'

Johnny: 'We were married for twenty-four wonderful years until my wife died. I did not think I would ever want to marry again. But three years on I love Alice in a special, but different, way. You don't think we are too old to have a big wedding, do you? That's what we both want.'

Fiona: 'When I married in my twenties I thought that was the end of the chapter. Now, fifteen years on, I am marrying again and see it as very much the beginning of something, and of a precious "something" which needs caring for and nurturing.'

If only we'd known ...

'Well, as they all say, if only I had known then what I know now. With the wisdom of age – I am thirty-two – I can see that at seventeen I wanted a wedding, and then looked around for the chap. We were both too young, so there are no hard feelings between us. This time I have found a terrific guy and want everyone to celebrate our good fortune with us on our wedding day.

Are there any rules?

Many couples find themselves in a dilemma about whether or not there are any rules which should govern the celebration of a second wedding. Is there a right way to go about a second wedding? 'Etiquette' may seem an old-fashioned word, but remember it only means a conventional code, and its purpose is to give people guidelines regarding behaviour, in other words, to help everyone to feel comfortable and to know what is expected of them on a social occasion.

The age old dilemma of 'what will people think' still haunts many of us today as it always has done. However, the emphasis has changed and the focus nowadays is not on which knife or fork to use, but on wanting to ensure that no one is hurt – for instance, ex-in-laws and children of the bridal pair, if there are any – and on wanting to ensure that a hundred other tricky situations are dealt with in a sensitive and thoughtful way.

> Anyone who has ever planned a wedding knows that it is full of pitfalls for the unwary. Something which seems to be straightforward is in fact much more complicated.

A popular TV programme, *Weddings from Hell*, showed video clips illustrating just how many calamities can befall the unprepared. It may make good TV viewing, but while we look with horror at the bride who trips up on her veil or the groom who knocks over the cake we all cross our fingers and hope that these are the kinds of things which happen to other people and never to ourselves. However, accidents apart, there are numerous problems and points of detail to confront the bride or groom of a second wedding. Like any other social event, a wedding will only unfold smoothly if sufficient care has gone into its preparation.

Public attitudes to marrying more than once have changed greatly over the last fifty years. Our grandparents probably did not know of anyone who was divorced, let alone remarried. Only the occasional widow or widower was likely to have had a simple religious ceremony for a second wedding attended by a few close friends and relations. If there had been a divorce, the best that could be hoped for was a quiet civil ceremony. But the times have changed, and today men and women getting married a second time want to marry in style, so second-wedding celebrations are booming in every sense. Perhaps the one time when a quiet wedding is best is if you are remarrying a former wife or husband. In spite of a French writer, the Duc de Lévis, claiming 'We can love more than once but not the same person' this does happen more than you may think!

We are bombarded in the media with photographs of stars marrying and remarrying with all the trappings of a Hollywood film set. Bridesmaids in black? Already done by Liza Minnelli with her large entourage of women all of 'a certain age' ranging from twenty-six to seventy-eight years old. For this star-studded wedding the cast was complete with Liza's stepfather (the bride's mother's third husband) arriving with his wife, a woman young enough to be his granddaughter. The press kindly described the bride, Liza, as 'a marriage veteran'.

'There's going to be a wedding!'

All the world loves a bride, and even the most unlikely people find they turn their heads at the sight of a bridal car; their footsteps slow down so that they can take a peek at a wedding party emerging into the street.

The excitement of a wedding day touches so many people. 'I'm going to a wedding' is a wonderful excuse to dress up, and everyone who joins in the celebration soon gets swept away by the joy of it all, even previously confirmed bachelors and unmarried women begin to think that perhaps there is something to be said for the ritual of a marriage ceremony. The occasion encourages couples who have been living together for years, to think that making a declaration of their love and commitment to each other in public does have a point after all.

> The old expression that 'one wedding makes another' has a great deal of truth in it.

So on this happy day, why is it that often there are silent tears wiped discreetly away as the couple make their vows to each other? Is it that the effect of two people vowing to care for and to love each other against all odds arouses a surge of trust and purity in this world of ever-increasing divorces? Can it be that for those who are married already, the ceremony calls up the memory of their own wedding vows and reminds them of their blind faith in the future – and in each other? Is this the reason for the hidden tears? Of course, for those whose experience of marriage has not been a happy one there can be wistful heartache thinking of what might have been, as they toast bride and groom and wish them all the luck in the world for their future together.

'Here comes the bride!' This phrase has a magic ring about it, from the time the five-year-old girl playing at weddings dresses up in her mother's net curtains, to the moment when the congregation hushes as they catch their first glimpse of the bride walking up the aisle. But what if it is, 'Here comes the bride … again!'? A *second* wedding day is just as much a day of hope and trust as a first, and therefore an occasion just as special. As I have already said, there are more issues to consider than were on the agenda the first time round and in later chapters we will take a look at them.

But, the first thing to keep in mind is that this is *your* special day, and with a lot of planning, and a bit of luck, it will be a day to remember and a wonderful beginning to a happy married life.

Once you have made the decision to get married again, where do you begin?

If only we'd known ...

'I didn't realise a second wedding can leave a bittersweet aftertaste. You can't leave out memories completely.'

Begin at the beginning

The love you have for each other and the private promises you will have already made together is an excellent starting point.

It is important to get off on the right foot. Once you and your partner have decided to 'go for it', then it is time to draw up an action plan together. I almost wrote *battle* plan, because after a while this is what it might feel like as you are faced with an endless list of things to do and to sort out.

Believe me when I say it is very, very important for you as a couple to keep a sense of proportion and not to lose sight of the fact that a wedding day – however important – is just that: a wedding day. See it as a gateway to happy married life. By all means do all you can to make it a lovely, happy and exciting day, but don't let yourself become so enmeshed in the ups and downs that you get exhausted and irritable with each other, allowing a dark cloud to overshadow your happiness together.

> Don't be like Len and Clara who became so overwrought they wondered why they had ever started on – in Len's own words – 'this wedding lark'.

Before you tell everyone the news, the two of you should have already agreed on the plans you have for the wedding.

Finding the right person a second time

In this busy world it can be difficult to find the time to seek out that special person. With the hurly-burly of everyday life it is often not easy to give time to affairs of the heart. And, however hard it was to find the right partner the first time, you will find it gets progressively more difficult to get back into the marriage market a second time. I get as many e-mails from men as from women – although women find this hard to believe – with the same wistful enquiries: 'Where can I go to meet someone really nice?', 'Where are all the single men/women these days?', 'Will anyone want to get involved with me? I am a single parent with two kids...', 'Who would want me? I have three children who don't live with me, but whom I see at weekends. I'd love to marry again. I just never meet anyone.'

Men and women who are looking for a new partner are often at a loss about how to meet other like-minded people. So much time spent at work plus so much with the family or with children from a previous relationship, leaves little time to mix socially with new people. Moreover, after having been in a relationship for many years, the thought of seeking out a new partner can be very hard; panic can set in if there is nobody on the horizon at all.

> There is no shame in joining singles clubs or dating agencies – you may be surprised at how many of your friends have met their partners that way!

More people are now turning to social events organised for singles. And dating through an agency or through the Internet is gaining ground. Furthermore, this often works. I have heard from too many men and women who have found partners in this way to doubt that happiness can be found by these methods. Of course, a word of caution: anyone meeting a stranger for the first time should do so in a very public place. But, I am pleased to report that many couples have told me that they have found the person they are looking for and owe their happiness to 'the web' or to an organised singles dinner party or dance. Couples who do meet in this way are often shy at telling friends that this is how it came about.

> When meeting a stranger be cautious: meet in a public place or even take a friend, though preferably not one also on the look out for a partner!

One other thing – this may not be an issue for you, but I hear of it quite frequently! – you need to get your stories straight about where you met each other.

George told me: 'I am dreading our engagement party. What if someone asks us how we met? I *can't* say "the Internet!"' Why not, indeed? The question may be asked by someone who is desperate to find a partner themselves. If being asked where you met is going to cause you and your partner embarrassment, then it is best to get your story straight in advance! It is surprising how often life has a way of confronting us with the people who ask the very question we dread having to answer.

Bill found that working long days and spending hours on the road most weekends driving back and forth to see his children left very little leisure to form a new relationship. 'It takes time to get to know someone, and time is something I don't have,' he said.

David: 'I know I'm ready to date again. But I can't find anybody to go out with. I don't meet people at work, and married friends swear they don't know any unattached women, so what am I to do? Is an agency or a singles dinner dance only for "saddo's"?' My immediate response is 'no'; it can be very practical to go where you know the other people are not part of a couple either.

'Where did we meet?' laughed Richard. 'We don't mind saying…we met in Starbucks. Very twenty-first century, we thought.'

Jenny said that she almost despaired of meeting a new man. 'With three small children, and very little money I couldn't think where to meet someone. But I did. I looked in the local paper and read the adverts and one simply jumped out at me. I took all my courage in my hands and rang him. He sounded OK, but you never know. I was extremely cautious, but we did meet, and, well, now I am writing to you to ask your advice about planning our wedding!' Jenny went on to say that she was wary about telling friends how they met. But would meeting on a bus, or in the library, or at an evening class be so different? The days when we were 'introduced' to prospective marriage partners by our parents are long gone.

So why not use the Internet or even the local paper? It's nothing to be ashamed of, however much you might explain it away later: 'It started as a joke', 'I just left a message to see what would happen', 'Everybody's doing it' – these are all quotes from men and women who found love this way.

If only we'd known ...

'I can see it takes time to meet someone new. I
thought I would never fall in love again. It took
ten years before I did.'

'My parents would have a fit if I told them that I met
Johnny in a chat room on the Internet. What can I do?'
Joyce is wise to prepare what she is going to say if she feels
her parents will be appalled by the news of how she met
Johnny. Hopefully they will be only too happy that their
daughter has found someone to love and who loves her to
worry about such details. If not, she will have to spell out to
them how the dating game has been changed by the new
methods of communication available today!

Of course, as always with sod's law, it is often when we are
not looking for love that we are most likely to find it. Hazel
told me: 'I gave up on trying to meet someone. I decided to
get fit instead, so I joined a rambling club – and guess what –
I met the man I am about to marry.' So, if you find it difficult
to meet new people, join up for anything you can. Often a
shared interest brings the most unlikely people together.

If you want to get out and meet Mr Right or Miss Right or
even the ex-Mr or Mrs Right, get going! He or she is
unlikely just to knock on your door!

2

Getting married again

'The critical period in matrimony is breakfast time.'
A.P. HERBERT, *Uncommon Law*

Letting your parents and family know

The first thing to agree upon is who should hear the news first. Although it is customary for parents of the couple to be told about a forthcoming wedding as soon as possible, this is where things start being different for a second wedding. Before you tell *anyone* it is wise and prudent to stop and talk over together just how you visualise telling close family and friends.

It is likely that your parents will already have some idea that there is a romance in the wind. But, as I heard from Ellie, 'From the time of my divorce my parents kept saying they prayed I would find another man to love.' The reality turned out to be different. When Ellie went, with Gordon, to break the news her parents were incredibly uptight. Taking her to one side, they urged her not to rush into anything. 'What's the hurry?' they both asked, and pressed her to be absolutely sure before she got embroiled in further wedding plans. Later she could understand that they had been anxious to prevent her being hurt again, but at the time Ellie was distraught, as she had hoped they would match her own overflowing joy.

If only we'd known ...

'My father has been married five times, yet had the cheek to tear me off a strip when I said I wanted to marry a woman who has been married and divorced. My dad had the nerve to tell me it would never work.'

I have heard from many brides-to-be of this turnabout on the part of their parents. Indeed, Angela said that not only her parents but also friends and relatives urged caution and 'less haste'. They hadn't done this before her first wedding when she was eighteen. She told me she realised her family cared very much, which is why she didn't deter them from 'advising'. She went on, 'My father always used to say, "Unsolicited advice is worth exactly what you pay for it." And I think of this when everyone – including him – is trying to tell me what I must do.'

Katie, too, was taken aback by her family's 'abject hostility' towards a man they didn't know when she announced her wedding plans. 'I had been divorced for four years, and my future husband had for five years, yet my family were horribly rude, so much so that I refused to take my husband back into that snake pit.'

Understandably, couples find it very painful to be on the receiving end of family hostility:

'My own mother told me I was making a dreadful mistake, and my older and only sister is very jealous of me and very, very competitive. She has never been married and sees my second chance of happiness as totally unfair.'

If only we'd known ...

'My parents went ballistic when I said I was marrying a man who has three children. I thought they would be pleased, but they were full of woe and told me I would live to regret it.'

Lucy was in touch with me quite frequently in the run up to her wedding. Her parents found it very difficult to accept that their daughter was to be a stepmother and that they would, almost overnight, become stepgrandparents to three adolescents. Lucy said that her parents thought she was too young and inexperienced to know what she was taking on. Tempers were fraught, and it was an agonising time for Lucy when her mother and father said they would not come to the wedding. They would not meet up with the children either.

Eventually, Lucy had to take a stand and with tears tell her parents that her mind was made up. She loved Alec and his children and, although she would be sad if her parents didn't come to the wedding, she hoped in time they would grow to know and love her new husband and stepchildren. There was a dreadful silence for almost a week, and then Lucy's mother telephoned her to say that perhaps after all they were being silly and if Lucy could love these children, then so could they. It really was eleventh-hour stuff; they met up and after an awkward beginning, the plans already made for the wedding were discussed and Lucy's parents became involved.

Lucy: 'The heroes were the kids. They knew how much it meant to me for my mum and dad to come to the wedding. At the meeting they behaved impeccably and charmed my parents. I owe them for that big time.'

Betty: 'Please advise. I am thirty and plan to marry again quite soon. My fiancé is thirty-five and is also divorced. Does he really have to go to my father and ask permission to marry me? I want to do the right thing.' My answer to this is that I don't really see that there has to be any formal request for the hand of the bride. It is probably a good idea to let your parents know what is in the wind, and if they seem happy about it, then you can go together and 'break the news' to them. I am sure your parents will appreciate your sensitivity.

Of course, many parents are delighted at the news and the prospect of a son or daughter finding love, companionship and security again. They are full of joy at seeing how a broken heart can be mended.

Before you see your parents it is as well to have roughed out some plan about what you and your intended want in the way of a wedding, and even the part you want the parents to play. One couple told me that they each asked their parents to be the witnesses at their wedding, a role they all felt comfortable with.

Many couples are in a financial position to pay for their own wedding this time. However, fathers can turn pale at the thought of having to shell out for another wedding, so it is as well to have worked out together whether you are going to look for financial help.

Guidelines for telling parents that you are remarrying:

- If you are marrying a second-time bride, it may not be necessary to ask her father's permission but it is still a rather nice custom to visit her parents and tell them the news together.
- If you think there is going to be any dismay or shock from your own parents, it is wise to make an early visit to tell them what is in the wind.
- Before you meet with your parents decide whether you are going to ask them for a financial contribution towards the cost of the wedding.

Telling an ex

However estranged you have become from an ex-partner you should be the one to let him or her know the news of your remarriage. If you were the one who was dumped in the previous relationship, don't spoil it by gloating when you tell the news. Whatever the circumstances, the news should come from you and not from a third party. Don't be too surprised if the announcement is greeted by a variety of unexpected emotions! Even if your ex-wife or husband has already remarried they will be affected by the news on some level.

If your divorce has been followed by a true untangling of emotions and sufficient time has passed then hopefully your ex will feel settled enough to wish you a happy life with your new love. But don't count on it.

Some couples can genuinely wish each other well for the future, and maybe an ex-partner is sufficiently stable in the path he or she has chosen to accept the invitation to the wedding of a former spouse. Strangely enough, it is often friends and close family who find themselves embarrassed and uneasy about this happening. If either of you do invite an ex-partner or your former in-laws to your wedding, the correct thing to do is to introduce them by their name, not with the preface 'my ex-husband Ron'. Make the introduction as straightforward as possible: 'Let me introduce Ron'. Those who already know about your former marriage will be aware what the situation is, and it only complicates matters for those who don't if you go into a lengthy and possibly embarrassing explanation.

If only we'd known ...

*'When I told my ex of my impending wedding I was
totally taken aback. His immediate reaction was to
ask, "And will I be invited?" I said there was no way
I wanted him anywhere near me on my second
wedding day, and actually found no difficulty in
saying so. I thought it was an extraordinary thing for
him to say. He always could take my breath away,
and this time was no exception.'*

Connie wrote to me: 'I am appalled that my daughter Jane, who is remarrying next month, has decided to ask her former husband to the wedding. My husband and I find it most odd, and we still have strong feelings about the way he treated Jane. We wonder how we should greet a former son-in-law?' I only hope Connie can keep in mind that this is a joyous day for her daughter, and if Jane wants her former husband there and it is OK with the groom, then it is up to Connie and her husband to be sure there are no 'scenes'. A wedding is not the time to clear the air, or to settle old scores. At the very least, a polite chat – kept to the minimum if necessary – is all that will be required.

For Katie, a surprise came a few weeks before her wedding. 'His ex, who I get on very well with, asked if she could come to our wedding. I said yes, and then I got the barrage of "Oh my God! you want *her* there? And what if she

22

does something?" What if, what if? I panicked. She did come to the ceremony, but not the reception. I was told that she cried. She slipped out just before the end, hardly noticed.'

Andrea told me, 'We are marrying in a month and my partner thinks it is OK to ask his first wife to the ceremony and the reception. I don't want this, but don't know how to tell him.' There is only one way to sort this, and it is to say straight out that this is not what you want. Andrea's future husband may have no idea that this is causing a problem for his bride, although I would have expected him to check it out with her right at the start. This is *not* the time to grit one's teeth and stay silent. If the bride is unhappy with an invitation like this, then it should not be sent.

It is important to mention to family and friends before the day that you have invited an ex to your wedding, in order to prevent any unpleasant surprises. They will then be able to make up their own minds in advance about how they will handle the situation. It circumvents any possible shocks and unpleasant reaction on your special day.

Guidelines for telling your ex that you are marrying again:

- Make sure you tell your ex-partner about your forth-coming wedding.
- Decide together whether a former husband or wife will be invited to the wedding.
- If they are at the wedding, don't introduce them as 'my ex-husband/wife' – keep it simple.
- Prepare family and friends in advance for the fact an ex will be present at the wedding.

What to do about ex-in-laws

The same goes for ex-in-laws. Handling your ex-in-laws is nearly always a very delicate situation, especially if your former spouse has died. The news of your coming wedding may revive very painful memories for them as they recall your first wedding to their beloved offspring. So try to smooth the path for them as much as you can, and above all ensure they hear the news from you in a very careful way.

Jenny: 'I just don't know what to do. My husband died of cancer three years ago and I am getting married to a wonderful and understanding man. Should I invite my in-laws to the wedding?' This is a most frequently asked question which causes a great deal of anguish on both sides. I often hear, too, from parents who, while still caught in the grief of losing a child, are called upon to celebrate the remarriage of a son- or daughter-in-law.

As with any awkward situation, a face-to-face meeting is best. Before any invitations are issued a get-together, where you explain as gently as you can what is happening, is the kindest way forward. Your ex-in-laws' reaction to the news will give some indication about whether they would welcome a wedding invitation or prefer not to be present. If distance is a problem, a sensitive handwritten note in advance saying that you would love them to be there, but would understand if they would prefer not to be, will be appreciated.

Remember, too, they may fear this is the end of the road as far as your relationship with them is concerned, that a chapter is being closed. If you have children they may still be very much involved in your family life, and many grandparents have their hearts in their mouths at the thought of an ex-daughter or son-in-law remarrying and 'moving on'. So great tact and sensitivity is required here and hopefully some reassurance too.

Of course, even if you have been divorced, they may still be delighted to hear from you that you have found new happiness. You can be sure, though, whatever the circumstances, they will be pleased that you have taken the trouble to let them know, rather than just letting the news filter through on the grapevine.

Lauren's first marriage had been to a man from a very close-knit family. After the divorce she found that blood was indeed thicker than water, and although one of her brothers-in-law said he was happy for her and told her ex that the divorce was 'better than he deserved', she felt the family withdrew from her. 'I do try to see them, but it's not the same, they seem uncomfortable if I am around at a family gathering. I am not sure how they will take the news of my wedding.'

A frantic bride told me: 'Help! I never did like my in-laws when I was married to their son. Ten years on I am remarrying, and I have just heard via my kids that they are expecting an invitation to my wedding as they want to see their grandchildren as my bridesmaids. I don't want them!'

This is a tricky situation. To some extent it depends upon the size of the wedding. If it is to be a large reception, why not for the sake of the children let your ex-in-laws come? If you do, you are likely to get their undying gratitude. On the other hand if, like this bride you are planning a small, intimate wedding, then this could be your explanation to the children. Although it is not as good as the real thing, a photograph of the kids in their wedding finery would be very much appreciated by their grandparents.

If only we'd known ...

*'I didn't like having my in-laws at my first wedding,
and when I remarried I had to have them at the
reception because my children begged me to invite
them. As the reception was starting my now ex-father-
in-law dropped down dead in the doorway. I am sure
it wasn't deliberate but my goodness it put a damper
on the wedding.'*

**Guidelines for handling your ex-in-laws over
your new wedding:**

- Try to be the one to let them know about your forthcoming wedding.
- If you are a widow, or widower, and you would like to invite your in-laws, try to have a face-to-face meeting with them. This is the sensitive thing to do, as your wedding may bring up very sad memories for them.
- Their reaction will give you an indication about whether to invite them or not.
- If you have children from your first marriage at the wedding, but not their grandparents, be sure to send your ex-in-laws photographs of the children in their wedding outfits.

'Please advise me. My ex-daughter-in-law is remarrying and I have heard from a friend that we are going to be invited to the wedding. We feel it is inappropriate. Can we refuse?' If these ex-in-laws are uncomfortable about attending the wedding then a face-saving way out would be to write as soon as the invitation is received pleading a prior engagement. I believe this is where a white lie is the kindest way out of an unpleasant predicament.

Meeting the new *in-laws*

Throughout history brides have had a tough ride when meeting their husband's parents for the first time. Never has it been an easy encounter for any bride or groom. And it is likely to be even more fraught for a second wife- or husband-to-be. A very young bride will hopefully slip into another parental relationship with her in-laws, but this is less likely to happen if the bride has a more established identity of her own. There may also be awkward moments for a second bride if her intended's first wife is still in touch with his parents or they have painful memories of a much-loved and now lost daughter-in-law.

Sometimes, quite unintentionally, there can be hurtful incidents: for instance, brides can suddenly find themselves staring at a photograph of their fiancé's first wedding in a prominent position in his parents' sitting room; or a groom may be regaled by stories of his predecessor by his bride's unthinking mother or father. Couples can be hurt, too, as we have already seen if the parents' first reaction is less than enthusiastic about this second wedding.

Anna: 'I wish new in-laws of second wives would please stop talking about the ex-wife endlessly. They may be criticising her, but it still gets tiring real fast.'

Robert: 'My mother-in-law and father-in-law wouldn't decide if they were coming to the wedding. They said they might be busy, and obviously felt they had to make some kind of point. They came in the end.'

If you are the new bride or groom you must tread carefully as well. You may be meeting in-laws who have suffered from the divorce, or who are still grieving over the loss of their child's former partner. They may be wary about being too involved, and perhaps hurt again. It might be that they are not yet sure whether their child has made a wise choice. You might not like to think this is the reason for their attitude, but it may be the cause of their reluctance to welcome you wholeheartedly! Keep in mind that they may have readily welcomed into their family, and heart, their child's first partner, so it is going to take some time for you to earn your place in their affection.

'I have been married before, am now divorced, and have three children. My husband-to-be has not been married and his mother looks on me as a "fast feminist", which I am not, and she loathed me on sight. Is there anything I can do about it?' Well, there's both a 'yes and no' answer. This future mother-in-law may have reservations simply about her son marrying, let alone joining up with a woman with children! So you need to take it slowly, and with the interest of the whole family at heart, do your best to be friends with her. Play your part and don't talk too much about your ex when you are together. No one can ask for more from you. They will not want to hear about your previous marriage.

One mother-in-law is fine, but two? Irene said that her former mother-in-law, Jean, was still very much in touch, and was trying to slip into the role of mother-of-the bride for Irene's second wedding. 'I don't want to hurt her because she is still grieving over the death of her son, but this is a difficult situation.' It seemed Jean was assuming that she would play quite a large role – beginning with helping to choose Irene's dress – while at the same time Irene's new mother-in-law had also indicated that she would like to be consulted about wedding arrangements and Irene's dress! Poor Irene! I understood that she had very definite ideas about what she wanted to wear and the thought of having *two* mothers-in-law in tow when she went shopping was causing Irene's stress levels to rise considerably. I am afraid there are no very hard and fast rules for situations of this kind; it just has to be handled very sensitively, hopefully causing as little hurt as possible.

If only we'd known ...

'I wished I had known how much my new in-laws were still missing their ex-daughter-in-law.'

Remember the other in-laws too

Allan: 'I knew how much my ex-brother-in-law had suffered when my first wife was killed. He was a great support to me at the time. I decided to take him for a drink and tell him I was getting married again. It seemed the right thing to do, and I think he appreciated it. Later on I felt it was quite OK to invite him to our wedding.'

Belinda e-mailed me to say that her dilemma concerned her former sister-in-law. She was very uncertain whether to ask her to the wedding. The problem was eased by having a quiet lunch with her at which Belinda was able to tell Stella what was worrying her. It appears Belinda was right to have anticipated that this would be difficult for her ex-sister-in-law. A particularly acrimonious divorce had been hard on all the family, and Stella explained that she felt for her to celebrate Belinda's remarriage could be seen as a betrayal of her brother. However, there were no hard feelings on either side, and Belinda made sure that Stella was comfortable with a simple dinner to meet Jack shortly after the wedding, and the warm friendship between the women has continued. How differently it might have turned out if Belinda had either unthinkingly posted off an invitation, or felt too embarrassed to discuss the situation and therefore not invited Stella at all. Belinda's last e-mail to me was simple and to the point: 'Thank heavens I cleared the air. I wouldn't have hurt Stella for the world.'

Hannah wanted to share a problem she had with her future sister-in-law when her engagement was announced. 'My sister-in-law thought it was her "Christian responsibility" to inform us that we would never be recognised before God in our marriage. She also said that she and her husband wanted us to know that God would never forgive our divorces. It seems that mental abuse doesn't count.' This caused Hannah and her partner untold grief, until about a month before their wedding when her sister-in-law had a change of heart: 'She and her husband offered to sing at our wedding!'

If only we'd known …

'It came as a shock to us both that our families had their own strong feelings about our wedding.'

♥

How will your friends react?

Very likely you will find that friends as well as family will be delighted to hear the news of your forthcoming wedding. They will share in the pleasure of seeing you happy again, after what may have been a very difficult time for you. As Nicola reported: 'All my good friends asked me two things: "Are you happy?" and "Is he good for you?" Once they found the answers were "yes", they were behind us one hundred per cent and never looked back. They are thrilled for us, celebrated with us, and we grew even closer.'

Oddly enough the media are not always so kind to someone they have featured as a grieving widow or widower who announces they are getting married again. Just think of the reaction when President John F. Kennedy's widow announced her plans for remarriage to the Greek tycoon Aristotle Onassis. It was almost as if Jackie had betrayed the whole country by refusing to continue to be the icon of the suffering widow. Remember, too, the tabloids' attitude to Sir Paul McCartney? There were gasps of horror when he announced his plans to remarry.

Angela was at a loss to understand the reaction of her friends. All along they had wished she would find a 'good and kind man' this time but in reality they seemed less than pleased when she actually found one. 'It seems impossible for them to believe I am happy.' She was deeply hurt at their suggestions she was remarrying 'just because she was lonely' or 'at forty making one last try for a family' and, worst of all, when they insulted her by asking the age-old question, 'Are you pregnant, then?'

Charles, a widower, said that after his wife died people were so very kind to him. After a year he proposed to a close family friend and they decided to marry fairly soon. 'At our age I couldn't see the sense of waiting around. But, oh my, did disapproval come my way. It seemed that people liked my grieving widower role and, quite frankly, some people were quite horrid in the condemnation of my remarriage.'

Caroline: 'We don't want to upset anybody. We have been living together for some time but now want to marry. We are thinking about having the ceremony at our home, and a reception and dance at a local sports club. I am not sure if I should invite everyone to our wedding ceremony, or just a few to the ceremony and everyone to the reception. Do people get offended if they are invited to the reception, but not the actual ceremony?'

I cannot think that friends will be upset if Caroline goes ahead with these plans. She had already told me that they both have children and had waited until most of them were grown up, and that now they would like a simple, intimate ceremony. Her plans have been thought through carefully. The significant people – Caroline, Barry and their children – will be there for the important ceremony and will be joined later by guests who will celebrate their union. It is distressing to read that after waiting for so long, Caroline is still haunted by whether 'people' will be upset if they go ahead and plan it the way they both want!

If only we'd known …

'The hardest thing was going against all family and friends who said our second marriage would never work. There was too much against it. We were both divorced and both had children. We have had the last laugh though – next month we celebrate our silver wedding.'

Try not to be too upset if you come up against friends who criticise your plans, or tell you, 'You can't do that.' Be prepared! Anthea, unfortunately, was not: 'Oh, why do people have to be so mean? I came through a ghastly marriage and divorce, but when Frank and I decided to marry there was all gloom and doom around as soon as people heard of our plans.' Anthea found that friends and family all urged a 'quiet' wedding. 'Why should it be?' said Anthea. 'We both felt we had something to celebrate.' The tears came for Anthea when her mother showed her disapproval at the choice of Anthea's wedding dress. 'I chose a very pretty full-length cream dress, but Mum said that it was totally inappropriate, and a "nice" wool suit would be more fitting.' For Frank it was a first marriage, and Anthea said she wanted to look like a bride for him. The next struggle was over how many guests to invite. 'Again, everyone said it should be a small wedding. Why? Why? Why?' asked Anthea. Why indeed?

Good friends may need some guidance about what you want. Carol wrote to me to say: 'My best friend is getting married for the second time. They are planning a big white wedding and there is to be a large bridal party. I am to be Matron of Honour. Is it appropriate for me to organise a bridal shower for my friend?' This question is an example of a friend wanting to do the 'right' thing, but fearful of making a mistake. I think the bride has sent out clear signals that she wants to pull out all the stops in celebrating this marriage, so why should Carol not have a shower and enjoy the fun of planning a celebration for her close friend. I later heard again from Carol that her friend had thanked her with tears in her eyes for planning the bridal party for her. Up until then the bride had had doubts that her friends 'approved' of the fuss she was making and seeing their loving faces at her shower showed her that they were behind her one hundred per cent.

If only we'd known …

'When I wanted to have the wedding I had always dreamed of, everyone was against it. They said I couldn't have a big wedding. My husband-to-be had never been married and he wanted what I wanted. It was tough dealing with all the input from the others at first, but you just have to do it your way, especially if you are paying for it yourself.'

3

Children and a second wedding

'Looking after children is one way of looking after yourself.'

IAN MCEWAN, *Black Dogs*

Children must be kept in the picture

When and how you tell your children that you are getting remarried is one of the most important issues you will have to deal with. Most couples who are in love and who decide to get married want to shout the news from the rooftops, but if either or both of you have children from an earlier relationship, you *must* tread very warily at first. I have heard from several couples who have told me that before they felt it was time to tell the children they had to 'whisper the wonderful news to each other'. As one mother cautiously said, 'I thought we should put off telling his children for as long as possible.'

Briony came to the same conclusion from a different angle. She told me with an almost audible sigh, 'We wanted to be the only ones to be silently celebrating for a while. We knew that once we told the kids things would change, and we were right. From then on, we had to put them first.'

Walking on air and hoping that 'all the world loves a

lover' is a stance that can be swiftly shot to pieces by kids of any age, as many prospective brides and grooms will tell you. If the children live with you, and consequently have a grasp on all your social activities, they may already have a good idea of which way the wind is blowing. And it may not all be bad news. Some children embrace the idea of a wedding with tremendous excitement, and welcome the addition of another member of the family with open arms.

Some children cannot wait to be involved in all that a wedding entails, and breathless questions such as 'Can I be a bridesmaid?' and 'What will your wedding dress be like?' may come pouring out. But, unfortunately, not all children respond in this way. And as a result you may soon suffer the pain of realising that the people you love most in the world do not have any intention of loving each other!

> I cannot emphasise too strongly the great importance you should attach to this early preparation of how you get to know the children. As soon as you decide on a future together, you must give very careful thought about how and when to tell them your plans. The way this is handled can make a vital difference to the success or failure of the future family.

The hard fact is that this early stage is a crucial period in the life of the 'new' family that is about to come together after a second wedding; marriage between people who already have children is not the same as if they were both truly single. This may seem obvious, but what is often overlooked is just *how* different it is going to be. Marrying someone who is already a parent means that there are more close family members to consider at the time of the wedding than there would otherwise be. So be prepared!

Many couples are right to be alarmed by the statistics, which show that the majority of failed second marriages are those which include children from an earlier relationship. Preparation and a sensitive touch are essential.

A wedding is in the air

Are you marrying someone who has a child or children already? Are you a parent about to remarry? Do you both have children to bring to this relationship? There are different combinations of the players in this family merry-go-round, but it makes no difference: although children may have been happy enough to be involved in some family activities with a new person, the moment the idea of a *marriage* is mooted, the atmosphere is likely to change and the announcement of a wedding met with frosty indifference.

If only we'd known ...

'It never crossed my mind to be prepared for his kid to disapprove!'

Listen to Adrian, a forty-five-year old man who had not been married before, and who fell in love with a woman with two children: 'Too right it's complicated. I thought the kids liked me, yet when I told them I was marrying their mum, they went wild, and not with excitement. What can I do to get back to the old relationship?

Adrian later revealed that it was at a rather quarrelsome lunch that he announced the news 'seemingly from nowhere'. Adrian soon realised that he had a lot of lost ground to make up. He sensed the children now felt his attitude was 'You won't get away with all this arguing and rowing when I'm your stepfather.' This lasted for several months and whether or not this was what Adrian – unconsciously – was implying, we do not know, but something went wrong from that lunchtime onwards.

Celia: 'My boyfriend and I have decided to marry. He has a two-year-old from another relationship, and I would like to know what is the form here? Obviously she is too young to be told anything, isn't she? I don't want her at the wedding.' Adrian and Celia have something in common here; they both seem to have kept their fingers crossed and hoped against hope that the existence of the children would not impinge on the plans they were making. Nor would they take into account that a child might have feelings which are likely to differ from their own. How wrong they were. Adrian took a very long time to recover the lost ground and later realised how he and his fiancée should have talked over when and how they would tell their respective children. But *is* there a 'good' way to let the children know that a parent is remarrying?

You must remember that we are talking about children

who will already have had major changes in their lives. They will have witnessed the break-up of their family for one reason or another, and possibly the remarriage of one parent already. They may have had to move house, and school, and may be anxious at the thought of anything else which will alter their lives. And there may be an underlying fear and resentment that this new partner will demand even more time and attention of their mum or dad.

Although Adrian realised all too quickly that he had put his foot in it, and was trying to mend fences as rapidly as he could, Celia was unsure about what part her fiancé's child would play in their lives, not just on their wedding day. As so often, the e-mail sent to me appeared to be about an issue connected with the *wedding*, whereas it was really concerned with something much more fundamental festering away underneath, something much harder to put into words. What was Celia really asking me? Was she trying to find out just how much account she had to take of this little girl?

Let's look at this from the point of view of a man or woman who has become involved with someone who is already a parent. When I wrote my previous book, *Find Your Way Through Divorce*, I talked with many such parents and discovered how complicated it always seemed to be to decide when and where this new someone should be introduced into the children's lives, which is extremely irksome if you are the one who is longing to become part of this family. The consensus of opinion, though, was that the key to success was to give everyone time to get to know each other. This is something which can never be forced or hurried. And only *after* this core relationship has been established should the idea of a wedding be introduced.

The nitty-gritty

It is best to be together when you tell the children that you are getting married, as this gives them a glimpse of you as part of a married couple again and reinforces how important a decision it is. Don't dodge the issue by letting them somehow become aware that there is a wedding going to happen. And tell them in private; don't make an announcement at a family gathering or when there are other people present. It is probably best to do it in your own home, rather than during a meal in a restaurant.

If only we'd known ...

*'Ben and I had been living together for a year when
we decided to marry. Polly and Stephen, aged four
and nine, spent every other weekend with us. So we
didn't think there would be any repercussions when we
told them the news. Boy, were we wrong. Polly asked if
their mum could come to the wedding, and when I
said "no way" she burst into tears. I wish I had
bitten my tongue and said nothing.'*

After you have told the children, give them a few days to talk to each of you. They are sure to have questions, and they may need to be reassured again and again about whether or not any major changes will take place. If you do have plans which are going to bring about any sort of upheaval, don't skim over them. Bring them out into the open and spell out what is going to happen. If there are likely to be changes but you are not certain about them, say so.

Abigail: 'Jack has been divorced for five years, yet when we told his two children – who are seven and ten – we were marrying in the summer they looked surprised, and one asked, "What about Mummy?" I couldn't believe my ears. What do you think this means?' What it means is that like many other 'children of divorce', somewhere at the back of their minds there is the hope that their parents will get back together again, even against all the evidence. They probably have distant memories of times which were good, and somewhere an unrealistic hope that the clock will be turned back. The knowledge of a forthcoming wedding puts paid to such dreams and fantasies. So keep in mind that the announcement about your wedding is likely to be a severe shock to them.

Guidelines for telling the children you are getting married again:

- You should both tell them together.
- Don't make an announcement in public.
- Make time for each of them to talk to you.
- Be prepared for questions you may be asked about how it will affect them.
- Give them time to absorb the news.
- Answer their questions truthfully; don't try to pull the wool over their eyes.

Moreover, on being told the news the children may raise questions you have not even considered: 'Will we have to move?', 'Will he be moving in with us?', 'But is she Jewish?', 'Will we have to go and live in Canada?' So again, do your homework before you tell them. A comment which took Rose's breath away was when her thirteen-year-old, who had listened calmly to the news, then said; 'Oh Mum, are you sure?' Rose looked at Stan and burst into tears. 'Of course,' said Rose, 'in a way I was sure, but it was hearing the serious way that she asked me, which made me have second thoughts.'

'I'm not coming to your wedding!'

What if one child is thrilled and another goes into a sulk? This is a common occurrence, and one which needs tactful handling. Don't try to jolly the one in a strop out of it without first working out what it is all about. It may not be something to do with the news. Averil was devastated when her sons appeared to be against her marrying Robert. When you are hoping the news will be a cause of celebration it is a great disappointment to be met by one or more faces with cross or glum expressions. Only later did she discover that the date that they had decided upon coincided with a very important sports fixture! There were sighs of relief all round when the date of the wedding was altered.

Keep in mind that although you and your partner have been aware of your future plans for some time, the news of your getting married may come out of the blue for the children, and they will need time to digest it. They may want to talk it over with their other parent, or grandparents.

So give time for the dust to settle. It is quite likely that a child will worry that showing approval of the union and taking part in the ceremony will be seen as betrayal of their other parent. Hopefully your ex-spouse will not put a spanner in the works, and if the children need 'permission' to enjoy themselves this will be freely given. So be patient with them, even if you are longing to firm up your plans.

If only we'd known ...

*'We told them together, set the scene, and Lily jumped
for joy. Then when she saw her sister's sour face,
stopped and looked sulky too. I could have wept. In
fact, later when the children had gone out, I did!'*

Helen found she was in for a hard time over the next few months. Lily was so influenced by her sister that she too refused to cooperate. When talking to the girls' father Helen soon understood that he was still very much against his ex-wife remarrying. He had told his daughters, time and again, how a new stepfather would want to take over, and probably push him out and prevent him from seeing them. So, before she could begin to bring the girls around to the idea of a wedding, she found she had to talk and talk with her ex to try to get him to help the girls accept the inevitable. 'Luckily,' said Helen, 'I was marrying a dear man who was long-suffering and was prepared to wait until the girls were ready.' At the beginning

44

they had no idea how long it would take. Helen's ex was reluctant to change his position and to encourage his daughters to welcome the idea of their mother's remarriage.

Even if you 'go by the book' and plan each stage carefully you have to remember children can be very unpredictable. Geoff and Harriet thought they had it all planned out, even with a bottle of champagne cooling in the fridge. When they told her four children together, the three eldest whooped with delight, while Adrian burst into tears and ran from the room. They didn't feel it was right to go on celebrating, even though the other three were bursting to know details of the wedding. It took Adrian a long time to come round to the idea of his mother marrying again, and it was a considerable period before he would talk once more to Geoff who up until the 'announcement' had been viewed favourably as a mate.

Geoff told me, 'Luckily I am a patient kind of guy. Others might have taken real offence at his attitude, but Harriet and I had time to wait until he came round. It showed us how much he still missed his dad who had died five years earlier. We should have thought of that.'

I have heard of children who were noncommittal at the beginning or even downright opposed to the idea, but who came round in time. They became intrigued by the preparations and drawn into the planning. But what if the resistance to the wedding goes on past the initial stages? There are some kids who refuse to take part at all. Even if on the surface they are baulking at the idea of attending, it is in the interests of the family of the future for them to be encouraged to attend. Not that this is always an easy thing to arrange. And it is a great sadness when this morose attitude of a child throws a pall over the wedding plans; not surprisingly, it can be hard for the parent and step-parent to keep even-tempered about it.

If only we'd known ...

'It is as if Roberta is trying to ruin my big day. She sulks and whines to her dad if we mention the wedding. I don't want her there, anyway.'

Jeannie told me: 'We are about to tell Josh's kids we are getting married. Oh, *do* I have to have them at the wedding? They live with their mother and will spend every other weekend with us, worse luck. After all, I don't see what it has to do with them. It is our day.'

Like Celia, whom we heard from earlier, brides like Jeannie were honest enough to say they do not want a child from a previous relationship of their partner to be at the wedding. So it is not always the child who is reluctant to include a new parent. It can be the other way round. However, a real word of caution here. What has been learned, not only from child psychologists but also from 'adult' children who can remember the remarriage of a parent, is that if a child does not witness the marriage they will never truly accept that it has happened. This is not a good beginning to family life.

A leading question must be why should someone not want a future spouse's child at the wedding? Is there some denial of reality going on, perhaps on a subconscious level?

A refusal to admit that there has been a previous liaison, let alone an offspring? Has there been a full discussion about future involvement in the child's life? Will the child be living with the new couple, either full- or part-time?

Barry found that when they gave the news to Alan, the seven-year-old son of his future bride, he seemed very much against the whole wedding idea. So what Barry did was this. When Marie was working late, Barry took Alan out to supper, in itself a great treat for this little boy. He asked Alan if he would come along to buy the ring ('You know Mummy best and I want to make sure I get the right one...'). Alan now felt truly involved and there was no stopping him. Barry told me later that at the wedding service they added a vow which included the words 'Your child becomes my child ... and my love for you and your child is pure and unshakable ...'

'There was no way that Chris, my fiancé's fourteen-year-old, was going to be included with the wedding organisation. He was sullen, and would not get involved at all. It was three years later, when I had really got to know him, that I talked to him about the way he had behaved. He managed to blush and to mumble that he remembered how he was. He has matured, I suppose. Tell other couples to just plough on ahead and ignore the child who won't take part.'

Many parents have suggested: 'Do it in stages. First of all, let the children see how much you love each other ... then get engaged ... and *then* tell them about getting married. Include them in all the planning, and begin to talk about "our" wedding day, meaning the whole family. Don't be too hasty. Take time.'

> For as many kids who are thrilled to be involved with
> selecting their wedding outfits, there are those who will
> say, 'I am not dressing up!'

It goes without saying that you should do everything you can, obviously without putting undue pressure on them, to encourage the children to be involved. There are some wonderful ways that children can be part of the wedding day itself, but you may have to compromise on some issues – perhaps in the way of dress. What if some of the children want to wear wedding finery of your choice, and others do not? Wise couples decide not to make a fuss about this, and try to avoid a major row. After all, children do like to make a point. What will you have gained if you force a reluctant adolescent into a dress when she only ever wears trousers? If you back off, you may get her grudging respect. Remember, you can usually find a way to avoid a head-on collision. Perhaps this unwilling child will be only too delighted to sit at the back of the church, and not be part of the bridal party. If so, is it so terrible? One tip here, however. If you can, have a photo taken to include you all. It may become very important in later years for the child to see that she *was* included, and that even on your wedding day you made allowances for her taste in fashion.

Marnie: 'Can you help me? We both divorced our partners to be together after a long affair. His kids do not want anything to do with me, so how does he go about telling them he is going to marry me? We know they won't come to our wedding.' With some difficulty, I suspect, but it is something

48

which must be done, and done in good time before the wedding day. The key to all this is to acknowledge that this second wedding is going to have some sort of impact on the children. This may not apply to adult 'children' quite as much as to little kids, but it is going to affect them all the same.

Let's be honest and acknowledge there are brides and grooms-to-be who are less than willing to be involved in telling their partner's children about a forthcoming wedding. But this is a job for you both to do together. Do not trick yourself into believing that they are either too young or too old to be affected by the news of the remarriage of a parent. However impatient you are to get the show on the road, be guided by the parent as to when and where you will tell the children that you are getting married. *Do not harbour any illusions that the children of your intended do not matter on this day of all days.*

Advice for parents who plan to remarry

It is always a big step to decide to marry, and an even bigger one when you have children to consider. How you interpret a view, so it is said, depends upon where you are standing. If you are a parent considering remarriage, it can often be quite daunting, but if all goes well there is no reason why it shouldn't be exhilarating.

If you have been a single parent for some time, it may have had the effect of strengthening the bond between you and your children; adversity often binds us closer together. You may have taken a long time to fall in love again or to make up your mind to remarry. In this situation both child *and* parent may be scared of this tie being loosened when there is someone new on the scene. But, when the decision is finally taken, you will want to tell the children and to involve them in your plans.

Amy was anxious about this: 'I have been married before and have three children. I am dating a guy who has never been married before, but we are talking about getting married. Would love info on what's appropriate for a second marriage and how to handle my children. They love my boyfriend but have no idea that I would consider getting married. They think if I get remarried it should be to their dad. So it's a touchy situation.' An all too familiar scenario, I'm afraid.

Bonnie: 'My kids are adolescents and took the news OK. They teased Pete because he has not bought me an engagement ring but that was the only unexpected reaction.'

If only we'd known ...

'Tell parents to think in advance about what they are going to say. We told my boys and they jumped for joy, and then asked what would their jobs be on the wedding day? I wish we had thought it through and struck while the iron was hot.'

'I have a son of twelve. I want to remarry. My boyfriend says he would like to ask my son's permission. I am not sure about this. What do you think?' This question stopped me in my tracks. I don't think it is a good idea to pretend you are asking the children's permission to marry. It is obviously not true, and besides what if they say 'No'? Even if they say 'Yes', it puts too much responsibility on the children. What if things go wrong? How will they feel when you have the usual family squabbles? I understand the lines this husband-to-be is thinking along, and admire him for being sensitive to the boy's feelings. However, a serious 'grown up' discussion with the twelve-year-old would surely be better, and the boy's 'advice' sought over less contentious issues.

Elaine: 'After being a single mum for five years, I couldn't believe how lucky I was to find a good man to fall in love with. He said he was happy to have my children as well, but it is a huge step to take and I dread telling them.' I do wonder why Elaine uses the word 'dread'. Because by the sound of it they have all taken time to get to know each other, and she is not introducing David Copperfield's dreaded stepfather, Mr Murdstone, is she?

Sebastian: 'My daughter of eighteen would like to be a bridesmaid at my wedding. My bride is only three years older than my daughter. Do you think this would look odd?' What is Sebastian really asking me here? If the daughter and the bride are happy about the wedding plans, what is worrying Sebastian? Is it that we are back to the old question of 'what will people think?' In this case, that Sebastian is marrying a woman young enough to be his daughter? Several e-mails later Sebastian revealed that this was indeed the case, and he told me he felt enormous relief in 'talking' about it. He said he had not dared to put it into words with friends in case they were laughing at him behind his back.

A more complicated scenario is where a parent does not live with the kids, and has a life quite apart from them. The children may not even know that Dad or Mum is dating, and it is then that care should be taken not to jump the gun and make first introductions simultaneously with announcing marriage. Try to arrange a time for you to tell the children that you are 'seeing someone', and then for them all to meet up, if at all possible, and then for you and your intended to tell them the news together.

Even if the children are adults, and have children of their own, the news that a parent is remarrying will still cause emotional upheaval. They may be mature enough to greet the news with delight but, as with most things concerning second weddings, don't assume anything. Tell them together in a straightforward way, and outline something of what you have in mind. If distance is a problem, then a sensitive letter will have to do instead. Don't send a jokey e-mail, as this may not go down at all well. And don't even think of only telling them after it is all over.

A surprisingly large number of men and women said to me that they only heard of a parent's wedding 'by chance' or were told 'long after the event'. Even if a parent is estranged from his children it is cruel for them to find out in this way.

Every single child in this position who e-mailed me, has told me that even years on they felt grief about not being told that a parent was about to be married. It will also add fuel to the fire of resentment if they feel they were totally excluded.

What if you both have children?

This is an even more hazardous situation which needs very carefully handling. Depending on how friendly the two sets of children are you will have to decide whether to tell them independently or all together. If you settle on telling each family separately, then be sure to do it in quick succession. Nothing can make temperatures rise more rapidly than a resentful, 'Oh, we have known for ages that they are getting married.'

If only we'd known ...

'We told her kids and my kids at the same time. Mine were fine about it, but I can't say I like her two very much. They are too much like her vindictive ex-husband. If they want to come to the wedding, fine. If not ... they shouldn't show up.'

Remember that it is not a competition, and that if one set of children takes to the idea more generously than the other, it may be for unexpected reasons. Who do the children live with? What is your relationship like with the 'other' parent? How well do the children know you?

Helen: 'My daughter, who is sixteen, took the news so well, but Mark's son, who is the same age, said he thought the idea was gross and to count him out.' Try not to be too hasty and to see this reaction as final and as a total rejection of yourself. Avoid dividing the kids into 'good' and 'bad' here. It could be that sixteen-year-old boys are not so turned on by the thought of a wedding, and so Mark's son needs to be gently coaxed into the plans. It is surprising what a little bribery can do, as I heard from Leo: 'My son was *so* against our wedding. But when I casually mentioned that he could be kitted out in morning dress he "allowed" himself to be persuaded to go along with the plans.'

Cassidy and Paul used the same strategy: 'There were long faces all round when Paul and I broke the news to our children – ages ranging from six to nineteen. However, when Paul and I began to discuss aloud our rather elaborate plans for a posh wedding, they brightened up considerably and added ideas of their own.' Rather sensibly, Cassidy and Paul listened to their (sometimes outrageous) ideas and solemnly considered each one. 'Before long,' said Cassidy, 'they were taking over, and later Paul and I congratulated ourselves for the way we handled it all.'

Olivia: 'My fiancé has five children and I have two. We told them altogether. The children struggled a bit with the news, even though I have been divorced since 1980. My fiancé's oldest children said they would come to our wedding, but only to keep their father happy as they are struggling with the idea of our marriage at all.' Olivia said that it was hard on her stepchildren-to-be because their mother was making a huge scene, saying the kids could have stopped the wedding if they had only refused to meet Olivia. Knowing the pressure they were under made it easier for her to understand their reluctance to participate.

'Be prepared for anything' was Phil's advice. Although Phil and Sara had been living together for four years they had never married. When they told their kids that this was what they were planning to do in the summer they were both stunned at Phil's daughter's reaction. 'Aren't you married?' she cried. 'But you have been *sleeping* together all this time.' Phil and Sara were lost for words.

'My kids will be at our wedding, but his will not. Mine are younger, and as it is term time his are away at college. That's OK, isn't it?' As always, I ask myself just why this question is being asked at this time. If Joan felt entirely happy about the arrangement, I don't think she would have written to me. Or perhaps it is her future partner who is uneasy about the way this is working out. I do think it is a great pity that all the children cannot be present for the reasons I have already given. I do wonder if it is wise to plan a wedding at a time when it would make it difficult for all the children to be there. This couple should be prepared for difficulties ahead, especially if they are harbouring any hopes of blending their families together. I wonder, too, if the older children have been consulted? Just because kids are away at college does not mean they do not want to know what is happening at home. And the wedding of a parent is a big event, whether you are two or twenty-two.

Jan and Mike found they were holding their breath when they told their kids they had decided to marry. Both boys hardly reacted at first. Then they heard the magic word 'cool'. Heads nodded in agreement. Both parents breathed a sigh of relief, because they knew there was no higher mark of approval from adolescents.

Lindsay told me they both had ups and downs with their children over wedding plans. Yet on the morning of the day she found a card pinned to her door: 'For a loving mother and her special man on their wedding day.'

Of course, if there are cheers all around, and I hope that there are, then you can move on to the exciting planning stage and work out together how and when the children will be involved on 'the day' (See 'Children at the wedding', page 174).

If only we'd known ...

'I was so concerned about Fred's children I forgot to keep an eye on my own. Big mistake!'

PART TWO:

Wedding Bells Are Heard Again

4

Planning the Wedding

'All weddings are similar but every marriage is
different.'

JOHN BERGER, *The White Bird*

Is a formal announcement necessary?

This time around you may feel you are not so constrained
by convention, but if you want to announce your
engagement or forthcoming marriage in the traditional way
with a paid item in a newspaper there is nothing to prevent
you doing so. This can be an announcement from the
parents of the bride just as it is for a first wedding, especially
so if it is in fact the first marriage for their daughter. One
announcement I saw recently took this form:

Mr and Mrs James Smith [the parents of the bride]
announce the news on this day of new beginnings
when their daughter Ann weds Mr Harry Jackson [the
groom-to-be].

So you really are free to decide on your own wording. On
the other hand, if it is a second wedding for both of the
couple they may prefer that the announcement is made as
coming from themselves:

Mrs Fiona Smith and Mr Harry Jackson
announce their engagement [or forthcoming marriage].

However, you may feel a formal announcement is not necessary at all and that an e-mail or fax to close friends will do the job just as well. You may like the idea of posting the news on the Internet; several websites devoted to weddings offer the space to do just this; you may even like to have your own website designed.

Take a look at www.virtuallymarried.com. This site offers a package which includes all the personal information you may want to post on a site, including photographs. The information will help you to create each page of your website. There is a free trial before you need sign up to this site.

All the same you can be sure of one thing: a new ring on your finger will make the announcement of your forthcoming wedding with the speed of light. Some couples like to give a party at which they spring the news on close friends. Several couples told me that this time around they chose to give their own engagement party.

Janice: 'We just thought, oh let's make it fun this time, and we sent a jolly invitation to a barbecue, hinting that there would be a surprise announcement. And our friends were surprised and on the whole very pleased for us. It turned out to be some party!'

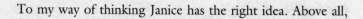

To my way of thinking Janice has the right idea. Above all,

do make sure you retain the sense of *fun*, at least in the preparation stages. Why shouldn't the second-time bride or groom have as much fun and excitement as possible over the engagement, for instance in choosing the ring? Some of the more mature brides-to-be wondered if they were 'allowed' to get engaged at their age. Why ever not? Romance is not only for the very young, and a period of engagement can be a wonderful time of preparation for a happy married life together.

If only we'd known ...

'Have a "mock" ring fastened to the ring pillow for a small boy to carry. We didn't and we all ended up on all fours under the pews searching for the ring which flew off the pillow as we walked down the aisle.'

If you are a widow you may still like to wear your first ring, but now moved to your right hand. If you are divorced and you have a daughter already, you may prefer to keep your first engagement ring to pass on to her later. Alternatively, there may come a time when you have the stones put into a different setting.

One bride-to-be had her own solution. Janie told me: 'I sold my first engagement ring to help pay for my second wedding. But I didn't tell anybody!'

Should I have a bridal shower?

The bridal shower, a long celebrated event in the USA, is only just becoming popular in the UK. Again, I have received a number of enquiries into whether it is 'suitable' for a second-time bride. I think it is a lovely opportunity for a party, and for the bride's women friends to celebrate with her. Even so, the thought of a shower can cause anxiety.

Jackie: 'I know that where I work, in a large office, they are planning a shower for me. Is there anything I should or should not do? I have never been to one. Does it mean I will have to invite them all to my wedding?'

No, Jackie does not have to invite everyone who comes to the shower to her wedding. There is nothing much Jackie has to do – just turn up and enjoy herself. But don't forget that brief thank-you notes, or even e-mails, for the gifts are always appreciated, and of course a special letter of thanks to the friend who organised the shower.

As many second-time brides already have a home with china and linen and all the usual things, an alternative 'theme' for the shower is often suggested. Olivia came up with the bright idea of having a garden shower. Knowing her friends were leaving their flats and moving into a marital home she suggested the guests brought items or tools for the garden, which gave much pleasure to the bride. But, there are any number of different themes – one of my favourites is a 'wine' shower. Although showers are not a necessary part of a wedding preparation, they provide an occasion for friends of the bride to let their hair down. The more mischievous of the bride's friends may suggest some games to play, or even give her some quite explicit sexual advice!

Grooms, I am told, seem to have 'upgraded' the traditional stag-night into an 'away' weekend, a custom not totally approved of by some brides, but apparently much enjoyed by the men they are marrying.

A new idea which is gaining ground for second weddings is a 'couple' shower. Perhaps these may be yet another excuse for a party, but they are becoming increasingly popular. The organiser decides on a focus which is reflected in the invitation, so that gifts are related to something which will be especially appreciated.

Jenny: 'My best friends are getting married and they have both been married before. They seem to have everything, yet I would like to give them a shower. Any ideas?' How about a gourmet food shower or something else which will force everybody to be inventive, such as a paper shower?

From time to time I hear from indignant friends and relations who believe that it is not appropriate for a previously married bride-to-be to have a shower. 'She has *kids*, for goodness sake,' said Lorraine. Well, Lorraine doesn't have to go, does she?

The older bride or groom

I am including this section because of the number of enquiries I get from couples who are in their sixties or seventies or even older, who plan to marry and very often have already been grandparents for some time. As people now live longer with improved healthcare, there is no reason why we should not see an increasing number of senior-citizen weddings.

Perhaps not surprisingly, this is the age range where there is the most uncertainty about the right way to proceed. There is the fear of 'looking silly at our age', the difficulty of 'telling our children', and a very heavy emphasis on 'What will people think of us?'

'How can I call myself a bride at sixty-nine?' cries one woman. Why not? In the eyes of your future husband you *will* be a bride on your wedding day ... his bride. And, if it's any consolation, did you know the word 'bride' comes from an old English word meaning 'cook'?

Why should there be a fear of 'looking silly'? Love can come at any age, and who said it is only the very young who can fall in love? Most likely the couple will be the envy of their friends; those who are intimate with them will be delighted that they have found happiness again with each other.

One groom-to-be wrote: 'Can you tell me of an appropriate toast for my wife on our wedding day? We are both in our seventies.' I believe there is no rule to follow here, and this man should just say what is in his heart, after which I am certain that everyone present will want to toast the health of the bride and groom.

Children can be distressed by their parents' remarriage, but this can happen at any age and hopefully more mature children will be able to cope with the situation. Unfortunately, more often than not things do not go as smoothly as they should.

Barry: 'Oh, do help us. My mother, a widow for years, is in her seventies and wants to marry again. She wants our children to be bridesmaids. How can I get it over to her that it is not right and it will embarrass everybody? I think they should just slip off somewhere quietly if they must get married, don't you?'

Well, no I don't. I think it is a charming idea to include loved grandchildren in the wedding celebration. What is there to be embarrassed about? Is it that Barry cannot accept that his mother may want a sexual partner or close companion? I can only hope that Barry begins to see the celebration for what it is, and can swallow his reservations and help to make his mother's big day a very happy family occasion. He doesn't seem to be objecting to his mother's choice, but to the fact it will be a public declaration of their union.

If only we'd known ...

'How could we have guessed our children would be
so fussed about our news? Our grandkids
were thrilled though!'

Lily, too, is another adult who was embarrassed by her parent's remarriage: 'My father, a widower, has been involved with this widow for years, and now they want to marry! What on earth for? What are we to do?' Again, I fail to see what the family crisis is about. It seems Lily has been happy for her father to have a relationship, but panic set in at the thought of marriage. And yet, many older couples who have had an 'understanding' for some time, do reach a point where they want to make it official, and to marry seems the right thing to do.

Fanny: 'I see you answer questions on your website about weddings. I love a wonderful man and he loves me, however we are both reluctant to get married because we think we are too old. What do you think? We are both pensioners. But I would love to be his wife.'

This last wistful comment – 'I would love to be his wife' – really touched my heartstrings. What does it say about society if this loving couple are reluctant to marry because of their age? No one doubts that there is something sweetly touching about a very young bridal couple, and I think there is the same surge of emotion when two people who are older seize happiness together in later years. No doubt Fanny would not want to wear the full finery of a young first-time bride, but she could look equally beautiful in a smart suit or some other 'dressy' costume.

I urged her to reconsider, and three months later I received an account of their wedding day: 'We had the best day ever. Lots of flowers, champagne and happy friends and family. I can't think now why we were so worried. We had a great honeymoon too!'

It can be a tremendous step for a man or woman who

was happily married for many years to think of marrying again after the death of a spouse. Jim felt quite at sea when he wrote to me: 'Jeanie and I have both lost loved partners of many years standing, but want to marry again for companionship, really. We just want a simple wedding ceremony, with no frills at all. Other people think differently and are not slow in coming forward with their disapproval.' It is sad that 'other people' cannot accept the sensitive nature of this union. I think this is one time when the couple should think only of themselves, and arrange to slip quietly away to have their marriage sanctified. It sounds as if they will have plenty of bitter-sweet memories on their wedding day, and they may feel like celebrating with friends some time later.

'May and September' weddings

What about a 'May and September' wedding? Again, why not? A seventy-five year old man can be just as vigorous as some men twenty years younger. And yet, these couples have their worries too.

Maddie: 'I am forty-six and have never been married. A darling man, who is twenty-eight years older than I am has asked me to marry him, and I have said yes. My worry is what to wear? Can I wear a long peach-coloured dress and flowers in my hair? I would like to.'

Yes, yes of course, the choice sounds perfect. What was it that had really been troubling Maddie? It emerged that she did not want to look 'too young' and yet wanted to dress in style for her wedding. A sophisticated dress in a fashion which flatters her should do very nicely – and I think flowers in the hair worn by women of any age are always lovely.

> Today it is not always an *older* man who marries a *younger* woman. Think of the film star Joan Collins aged sixty-eight who married a man thirty-two years her junior.

I do hear from women who are concerned about marrying a man who is much younger than they are. But what does 'much younger' mean? Some worry about a five-year gap, while others are fussed about a difference of ten or more years. The key issue seems to be that if a couple can grasp happiness at this point in time, accepting that it may be for only a few years, then why not?

What kind of wedding?

Planning a wedding is not for the faint-hearted, and yet in the UK we have not so far taken up the American idea of a 'wedding coordinator'. Those of you who have laughed your way through the film *Father of the Bride* will know how the wedding coordinator homes in on the family to persuade them to have all the de-luxe items that are 'necessary' for a beautiful wedding. Steve Martin – the father of the bride – is swept away trying to hold on to his wallet as the plans gather momentum.

In the UK the premier wedding coordinator is to be

found on the Internet at www.milestoneweddings.co.uk. Helen, the coordinator who spoke with me, told me that many of the weddings they are involved in are second weddings. According to Helen, second brides and grooms, while savouring the freedom to do what they like on their big day, also want to check out with a professional that it is OK to do one thing or the other.

She also told me, 'First weddings are bound by tradition, but for second weddings the couple are often glad to have the hassle taken out of all the planning. We do the lot, from sourcing venues to providing the confetti.'

Helen was keen to impress upon me that to have a wedding coordinator is not a luxury, but a boon in this busy and frantic world, and that they work on a fixed-fee basis too.

A wedding planner can save you time and stress. They will do all the running around, and negotiate with all your suppliers. If you feel daunted at the thought of checking over contracts and agreements and chasing up the people who have not replied to your invitations, then a wedding planner may be for you.

Getting married a little later in life does have its advantages: you will both have been to many weddings and probably already know what kind of wedding you would like yourself, and what kind of budget you have in mind. The very young first-time bride, with Daddy paying for everything, and Mummy knowing just what is best, often finds she has little say in how the plans take shape. Second-time brides or grooms picking up the bills themselves, and not trying to hold back on a budget for their parents' sake, may not feel so constrained this time around.

If only we'd known …

'Remember the old saying that every girl has
the wedding her mother dreamed of!'

Any bride who remembers her wedding as the 'happiest day' seems to signal that it was all down hill from then on! We should keep in mind too that for most first-time brides there is an enormous amount of stress and strain in the air. Happiest day of your life? Well, in fact not all brides would agree with that as they worry about whether it will rain, how the young bridesmaids will behave, or whether Great Aunt Hetty will get drunk.

I much prefer the comment that the wedding day was the 'happiest day … so far'. Recalling your first wedding may remind you of things which you wish you had thought of but which were not done. So, it is important to think through your memories of that day. It will help you to decide where you want things to be different. If you do not do this, something might suddenly remind you of your first wedding. Music, too, can be very evocative, so make sure you know and approve of any music being played during the ceremony.

If only we'd known …

*'I believed I had thought of everything, but then the
strong scent of the flowers reminded me of my first
wedding and to my horror I began to cry.'*

Second-wedding differences

There are many ways in which a second wedding is different
from a first. To start with, at a first wedding the bride is likely
to have the idea in her head that everything is going to be
'happy ever after'. At a second wedding, experience has
usually taught her that life is just not like that. But don't run
away with the idea that knowing this will make this marriage
work more easily – it won't. It may even be *more* complicated
and vulnerable because of earlier relationships, and especially
so if either or both of you have children already. You will find
that an ex-spouse who will not let go can cause endless pain
and conflict, so prepare yourself for this. Hopefully, being
forewarned will strengthen your determination that this time
you will succeed and have a happy and solid marriage.

Several couples have told me that they felt they had to
temper some of their joy to accommodate the feelings of
loss that others close to them were having: 'You have to
watch what you say and do so as not to offend people –
especially the kids.' 'We found that we could whisper our

joy when we were alone, but you can't shout it from the rooftops like the first time around.'

One of the major differences is that the groom is usually far more involved in second-wedding procedure. And a good thing too! Regardless of whether it is the bride or groom who has been married before, there seems to be much more of a feeling of planning 'our' wedding. I think this is splendid news. Many second weddings are planned by couples who are already living together, so it seems a natural development to do the organising together. They can have a lot of pleasure in making their wedding 'different' rather than going down a totally traditional route.

If only we'd known ...

'I have to laugh when I think of my first wedding. I was kept in the dark and on the day just got swept along by the arrangements. It was like taking part in a play where I hadn't even read the script! This time Sally and I are making sure that everything we want to happen, happens.'

Catherine: 'What kind of wedding do I want? Anything different from my first where we had three hundred people and the whole works. There was friction between my parents and my in-laws, and as I was nine weeks pregnant I felt sick. This time I just want to go somewhere quietly with Anthony and for us to become husband and wife.'

However, it is necessary to keep in mind that when this is a first wedding for either the bride or groom, there are probably going to be niggling worries about the previous 'big day' in their partner's life, and whether comparisons will be made by people present – including the couple themselves. I frequently heard of the dreaded phrase, 'What was your first wedding like?' So great care needs to be taken to make sure this wedding does not appear to be *second best* in any way. In any event, don't skirt around this with your partner. Any lingering feelings you may have that your soon-to-be-spouse is uneasy about any of the arrangements need to be out in the open. Any questions about what happened at a first wedding need to be answered truthfully.

Babs planned for them both to light a Unity Candle at their wedding ceremony. Fortunately, talking over the plans with her fiancé just a few days before the wedding, she found out that both of his ex-wives had done that at their weddings. So, no Unity Candle for Babs.

Remember that even the most laid-back and informal wedding has to be thought about well in advance. In fact, the more original and 'different' you plan to make it, the more you will have to ensure that all is in place and the preparation beforehand is swinging into action so as to make it a perfect day. Whatever you do, try not to leave *anything* to chance just hoping that things will turn out the way you visualise them in your dreams.

Rachel: 'Pass this on. Be creative about where you hold the ceremony or reception. We had ours at a grass picnic site at the back of an amusement park. We got permission to have a huge canopy erected, eliminating the worries about rain or shine, and parking was close. We hired two teenagers to come about an hour after we arrived to shepherd children to the amusement park, leaving the adults to enjoy a relaxing reception. I can just see what my mother's face would have been like if I had suggested that for my first wedding. My husband agrees that his parents would have had a fit too if this had been planned for his previous wedding.'

Arthur: 'My advice? Only second-time brides and grooms know the lay of the land. If the couple think they will meet animosity, I suggest eloping. That's what we did. Eloping isn't just for run-away teenagers, you know.' Other couples mentioned this: as the build-up to the wedding became greater they thought – not always jokingly – of skipping out of town, but the thought of what this would do to their families prevented this.

Ruthie: 'Do what you both want for the wedding. We had both tested the waters before, and previously we did everything according to the rules ... and our parents. Now it is our turn. We threw out traditions that seemed silly to us. We decided it was our party and we were paying. We told all the negative nellies to shut up and mind their own business. We had a wonderful time at our wedding. I don't think many first-time brides and grooms would say that, if they are honest.'

Who foots the bill?

With a first wedding there are established rules about who pays for what. But as with so many other things, when it is a second wedding the boundaries are not clearly defined.

There are, however, some guidelines. First of all, if the wedding is a first for the bride, but not the groom, it is usual to follow the age-old custom of the father of the bride being the host, and paying for most of the wedding expenses.

On the other hand, when it is a second wedding for the bride or groom, or for both, it is now the custom for the couple to pay for the wedding themselves. Although if your father wishes to contribute, ask him to tell you what sum he has in mind so that you know where you stand. If he is in a financial position and willing to do so, I am sure his gesture will receive a warm welcome. According to the website www.weddingguideuk.com, nowadays 'the average cost of getting married in the UK is around £11,000 with the vast majority falling between £5,000 and £15,000'. This may make you gasp, but you should keep in mind that *anything* which has to be paid for in connection with a wedding will cost more than you expect. As some couples found, it is as if there is a wedding surcharge which makes everything turn out to be twice as expensive as you would normally expect it to be!

Maxine: 'It's almost laughable what people think they can get away with. I made little tulle bags of sweets for my guests for next to nothing. The caterer had wanted to charge a fortune for putting them on the tables.'

If only we'd known ...

'I couldn't believe it when I agreed to ivy being
wound round some of the pillars in the room –
the cost came to four figures!'

Start out by making a budget based on what you can afford, and keep to it. This is more difficult than it sounds. Keep a firm eye on estimates from caterers, florists etc. Don't be seduced by 'We could add ...' or 'What looks very nice is if we did this or that ...' because these 'little touches' will *cost*. They are some of the things which can send your budget sky high. Keep in mind that the most enticing and 'bargain' offers are not always the best buy, since hidden extras and the small print may mean that a lot has to be added on.

If only we'd known ...

'At my first wedding my husband-to-be opted for a
"bargain" white limo. On the day a horrible looking
old car arrived. The driver said that the white
limousine had broken down. We discovered later that
this was a con and other couples had fallen for it. This
time I am having no "cash deals" but a contract
with a reputable car-hire firm.'

There are ways to keep down the cost, and these are mentioned in other chapters. For example, friends contributing dishes to a buffet reception at home, creating your own decorations, and ordering flowers which are in season. If you are holding your wedding or reception in a hotel, ask if it is possible to share the cost of decorations with the wedding or other function either side of yours. You may find a very willing couple only too pleased to do this.

Often the single most expensive item is the dress for the bride, but fortunately many encore brides are not tempted to blow the entire budget on a dress which will be worn only once.

If you are going to ask a friend to be your official photographer and video-man don't leave it all to chance. Although this will cut down on the cost considerably, take time to go over the details of what you think is important and exactly what you want recorded. Be upfront, and ask if your friend is expecting to be paid. Of course your friend might be delighted to do this favour for you, or as a wedding present, but don't take it for granted.

If only we'd known ...

'My best friend is an amateur photographer and asked if I wanted him to do our wedding photos. I agreed, but was bowled over to get a bill for £900 after the wedding.'

A thorny question is always who pays for bridesmaids' dresses. For a second wedding, if you are having grown-up bridesmaids or a grown-up matron of honour, they may offer to pay for themselves. However, it will probably mean they will want a say in what they wear. It seems to me that if you have definite ideas about what you want your attendants to wear, then the bride should pay for their dresses. Of course, if your children – or your partner's children – are to be bridesmaids or flower girls, you will all be in it together anyway!

Nobody *has* to go to and from their wedding in a limo – although this does seem to be a growing custom. Watch out for the outlay, though. If you want to travel in grand style in a horse and carriage or vintage car, your costs will rise considerably.

However, as you are most likely paying for the wedding yourselves, you will be free to choose just what you want, without having to look over your shoulder to see if your parents approve. Just make sure you get value for money, and you are not taken for a ride by any unscrupulous wedding professionals.

Whether your parents are contributing or you are paying for the whole affair yourselves, never give the impression to any suppliers or anyone you are hiring that you 'want the best' or 'money is no object'. This is the business side of organising your wedding day, so don't view any estimates with stars in your eyes.

What is a small *wedding?*

You will soon find out that one person's idea of a 'small, simple wedding' is not the same as another's! Even the word 'small' can mean different things to different people! To my mind 'small' means a maximum of twenty-five people, and probably even fewer, with just the wedding party and witnesses present. If you do decide upon this number, then be prepared for the shock horror of friends who may feel left out. Even believing that 'small' will include *them*, if nobody else!

> Alison : 'My husband-to-be had a huge first wedding. He wants us to have a small one, and I am very bothered by this.'

First of all, this bride needs to understand that *small* does not have to mean *dull*. Perhaps the man in her life wants this wedding to be more intimate and personal and there are many ways to achieve this. It is possible, for instance, to have an intimate ceremony with a few special people there, followed by a large reception. I urged Alison to talk and talk again with her fiancé, because to harbour resentment in secret about a wedding does not bode well for the future. This first step – for both of them – needs to be one they are both in agreement about.

I did hear later from her that the reason her future husband had desired a small wedding, with only very close family or friends present, was because he wanted this ceremony to be very personal to them both. Alison had mistaken the signals and was beginning to think that his ideas for the wedding were for a second-best affair, and she was relieved to find that this was far from so. The idea of a grand reception went down well with them both.

Roger: 'We agreed on a small wedding this time – I have been married before – but I have just been told that what my fiancée means by a "small" wedding is seventy-five people! I say it should be a maximum of ten! Who is right?' Well, in fact they both are. However, as it is a first wedding for the bride perhaps she can't ask fewer than seventy-five relatives and friends without upsetting a lot of people. Just think what she might have come up with if Roger had agreed on a large wedding! If he feels it is important to have only the minimum at the actual wedding ceremony, he should tell her this – and perhaps he can compromise by having a bigger party afterwards, or, if this doesn't feel right, at a later date.

> It is easy to forget that with a second wedding thought must be given to the bride or groom who has been married before. They will want to opt for something quite unlike what they had previously, and most couples marrying for the second time try to find a very different setting or style of ceremony.

I received a desperate cry from Ethan: 'A second marriage for us both. I had a small wedding the first time – we had no money. My intended had a huge first wedding. This time I want a large wedding which I can now afford, and Ellen wants us to marry in a simple fashion with no fuss. Advice, please.'

Some negotiation needs to swing into operation here. If there is a deadlock, then compromise must be the name of the game. A small, intimate ceremony followed by a grand reception?

Back came the reply: 'We hadn't thought of that. We can both agree to that. Brilliant.'

Pam: 'I was married with all the works. When that marriage collapsed I swore I would never do it again, but here I am considering it! This time it will be more low-key, where everyone is relaxed. I have learned that second time around it isn't worth spending money on material things. We will have lots of fun, but nothing formal this time.'

Laura: 'I need help with etiquette on my second and his first marriage. He is an only child of a mother and stepfather with a lot of money. Since his mother never had a daughter to plan a wedding for, she has decided to pay for ours entirely. I am very appreciative. My mother, on the other hand, does not agree with the kind of wedding we are having. We are getting married by the Justice of the Peace, in front of immediate family only. My mother says it is wrong that we are having a shower. I didn't ask for a shower! My mother and I have been arguing back and forth for months about all this. Shouldn't my fiancé, who has never been married, be allowed the benefits of a first-time wedding?'

I do wonder just why Laura's mother is so opposed to

this wedding celebration. It seems as if she is picking on the smallest thing – even a shower – to show her disapproval. It may be for religious reasons because she disapproved of a divorce, or she may regret that she cannot pay for the wedding and has little to do with the arrangements. Perhaps Laura could gently enquire what is really upsetting her mother, and then if all else fails, she must just tell her mother of the plans. No need to argue. No need to justify herself. These are the final arrangements.

Another surprise may be that one or other wants a religious service, while the other has taken for granted that they will have a civil ceremony. Even if both are in agreement about what kind of service they would like, it may still not be so straightforward.

If only we'd known ...

'I thought we had talked over everything. But somehow one important item slipped through the net: the size of the wedding!'

82

5

Where shall we marry?

SECOND WITCH: 'Where the place?'
WILLIAM SHAKESPEARE, *Macbeth*

A room with a view

You may want to go to pull out all the stops and get married somewhere unusual, like a country club, but it has to be licensed. And in the UK, remember that wherever you marry a registrar has to be available at the chosen place in order to register your marriage. We have not yet followed the United States where the star Robbie Williams transfixed the pop world by officiating at the wedding of close friends; in a space of just under forty-eight hours the top-selling rock singer was ordained as a minister and performed his first wedding ceremony! He received an on-line ordination and with his ordination certificate from a non-denominational ministry was able to officiate at a wedding. (In the US there are already Interfaith Ministries and a search on the web will find ministers willing to conduct inter-denominational weddings.)

> The law as it stands in the UK does not allow a civil marriage to be held in the open-air. There are government proposals afoot to extend the available settings even further, and the suggestion is that it should be the *celebrant* who will be licensed, not the venue. However, it is not expected that this will come into operation until 2005.

Perhaps you have already decided that you want a wedding in a church or synagogue, but otherwise you can let your imagination wander and consider whether you want to marry in a castle, or a museum or a theatre provided they have been licensed. A recent popular venue is the London Eye. Many second-time brides opt to have the same setting for the ceremony and the reception, something which is now much easier to arrange.

Whatever wedding service you decide upon there are people with the right qualifications to help you plan your ceremony. A visit to the registrar, priest, pastor, minister or rabbi will soon set you straight about what is and what is not allowed. Don't take anything for granted. Check it out first, particularly if it is something unusual. Let us take a look at what is possible and what restrictions there are for the different kinds of weddings which are normally available, and in particular how these affect second weddings.

If only we'd known …

*'Interview prospective clergy. Make them let you
read the entire service beforehand, so you
wont be surprised by what they have in
mind. Ask the clergy what they will
be wearing. We didn't and
still regret it.'*

A civil ceremony

There is not usually much difference between a civil service performed for a first wedding or a second, but in the UK over the last year or so giant strides have been made to extend the different locations where a civil ceremony can take place. However, there are legal formalities to observe and, as I have said, a marriage must take place at a registered or licensed venue. And for a marriage to be legal it must be a public declaration before at least two witnesses.

If you decide to marry at a registrar's office, you will find these are not the gloomy places they once were. Most registrars have gone to great lengths to create a pleasant atmosphere and you are sure to find the staff helpful and welcoming. A new and wonderful addition to some register offices is that a couple can have their wedding transmitted live by web cam! Just think of the pleasure this will give families separated by distance. 'It made me so happy to think my mum and dad could see it as it happened,' said Noreen, 'even if the time difference meant they were in their pyjamas.'

There is usually a restriction upon the number of guests you can have at a register office, so find out about this. Have a look around before you make your final decision and if videos and flash photography are likely to be used, make sure this is permitted. Ask if you can have some music and what is the best way to provide this.

The Superintendent Registrar will tell you about the original documents you will need, including a death certificate of your late spouse or a Decree Absolute if either of you has been married before.

You will find that there is usually a room for your wedding party to gather before the ceremony, and you will be called when it is time to go into the marriage room. Arrangements are usually in place for you to take wedding photographs afterwards. And make sure you do take them. There are some who do not think these are important when married for a second time, and later regret that there are no photographs to paste in an album. If you are not hiring a professional photographer and are relying on family or friends, it is a good idea to tell them beforehand what you would like.

If only we'd known ...

'No one took a photo of me with my dad on my wedding day, and as he died soon after I have always regretted that I have no photo of him with me as a bride.'

Ron: 'Don't leave the music to your younger brother. We did, and by mistake he played the wrong track for the CD. We were furious.' So, once more, check everything yourself.

Take note that most wedding parties arrive in a group, and as each wedding in a register office follows closely on the heels of the previous one, there is no leeway for the bride to be late! You may lose your slot.

Marrying in the United States differs from state to state. Connie: 'I guess we are lucky – a judge will marry us in a park in our hometown. No fuss, no frills, just a very relaxed ceremony.'

One last point: remember that once you have agreed on a provisional date, it can only be provisional until you have checked out the availability of the registrar. It is a shock for many couples to discover that while they have been so involved with their own wedding plans other couples have had the same dates in mind and have already booked up the church or hotel.

The Church of England and second marriages

The single most important major change for someone wanting to remarry in the Church of England is the recent decision made by the General Synod to allow divorcees to marry in church during the lifetime of a former spouse. Although ministers were allowed to use some discretion previously, until this was formally approved in 2002, there were some bishops who would not go along with it. Now it is entirely up to individual clergy, rather than their bishops, to decide whether to conduct a wedding for a divorced person. Some may still want to invoke a 'conscience clause' and are free to refuse if they so wish. But this change in the ruling will open the door to thousands of couples each year who wish to remarry in church. In addition, couples are no longer restricted to the parish where they live, so will be able to go to another church if their local priest refuses their request to marry. (This new ruling has come, of course, too late for some of the men and women who contributed to this book and told me of the grief and family strife caused by their marrying a divorcee.)

> George: 'I can't believe our luck in timing. We thought a wedding would be out of the question for us because we have both been married before and divorced. Then this wonderful news was reported. I think it is so clear thinking of the Church to move with the times.'

Some people fear that the Church is abandoning its stance that marriage is for life. But others feel that there is a need for a new approach, and that the demand for change was overwhelming. There has, of course, never been a problem if a widow or widower wants to remarry in church.

Juliette: 'My father didn't agree with the Synod's change of heart. He still says marriage is marriage. It will take time for some people to shift their views. So it is a civil wedding for us, even though we could now be married in church. Pity, really.'

However, it is not as straightforward as it sounds. Although the way has been opened for remarriage in church, a difficulty has been posed not just for some clergy, but for those men and women who made their vow to love their spouse 'till death do us part' in church at their first wedding.

Gail: 'I was married in church and it lasted for such a short time that I didn't really have time to see the video! Seriously, though, he left me three months after our wedding day. I am now deeply in love with Duncan, but I cannot marry him in church, it wouldn't seem right. After all, I made those vows and you just can't say them again, however well intentioned you are.'

Sally: 'I truly believed I made a vow not only to my husband but to God. I don't care what the General Synod now says, it has to be a matter of personal conscience. When I married Ben I had no way of knowing what was to happen, and when violence and drug abuse came into my marriage I had to leave, both for my children's sake and my own. It was not done lightly, believe me.' Sally told me that for her to consider a divorce had been a nightmare, and went against everything she believed in. However, when she subsequently fell in love with a man who loved her children too, she discussed her worries with a clergyman. In the course of time she felt that, although her promise at seventeen had been made in good faith, certain circumstances permitted a release from her vows. With some sympathy and support from her local minister, she felt she could make a promise to her new husband, and have the union blessed by God in church.

Sally told me: 'I would not have been happy with a formal civil wedding, and my second husband knew this. But it has to feel right for you, no matter what the "official ruling" is, and my local minister understood this. He had the same feelings about this very serious moral decision.'

There are some clergy who do not want to be seen as 'blessing adultery' and continue to do all they can to prevent the remarriage in church of a man or woman who has had an adulterous relationship which causes the break-up of a previous marriage. They hold on to their long-held belief that a second marriage is not allowed within the lifetime of a former spouse.

If only we'd known ...

'Tell people to leave their mobiles outside the church.
Wait for it ... a mobile rang when we were saying
our vows, and it was my husband's!'

If you have set your heart on a second church wedding, the only way for you to find out if an individual priest will permit this is to go and ask. It is not a good idea just to turn up in the hope that a busy vicar or minister will give you a few moments of his or her time, so telephone for an appointment. You will be asked some questions, so be prepared. Make sure you let it be understood you are talking about the marriage, and not just a wedding service in a setting which will look good in photographs.

Both of you should go along for the initial discussion, and even if the reaction is positive, you may find you will be expected to attend some marriage preparation classes prior to your wedding to show that you are truly committed to the idea of a wedding in church.

Statistics show that up until 2002, one in ten Church of England weddings already involved someone who had been divorced. For some vicars the decision used to rest upon who was the 'innocent' party in a divorce, but today innocence or guilt does not really come into the picture.

If you have any special requests about how you want the ceremony performed, now is the time to discuss it with the minister who will officiate. Some will welcome your choice of readings with passages or psalms which have a special meaning for you, and will let you make the service more individual in this way. Make sure you have thought through any changes you would like to have before you both speak to the minister. If you have children, then discuss the role you would like them to play in the service.

Brenda told me that although her local minister would not marry her again in church, she was quite agreeable to a service of blessing. 'I felt this really fitted the bill, and we were both happy about it.'

If it is not possible to be married in church, then explore the idea of a service of blessing after you have had a civil ceremony.

Service of blessing

In many cases, a blessing ceremony can be arranged with a vicar to be held in a church after a civil service, and many couples opt for this. There are also ministers who are willing to perform a service of blessing at licensed wedding venues. Once the registrar has completed the civil requirements, it will make the ceremony more personal with a blessing of the marriage.

When Brian and Pat, who had both been married previously, wanted to get married to each other, they found the best solution for them was to have a civil service, with a service of blessing afterwards given by both a rabbi and a minister. 'We both felt that was the right thing to do,' said Brian.

Roman Catholic weddings

Just as the Roman Catholic Church does not recognise a *civil* marriage, it does not recognise a divorce which is the *legal* way of ending a marriage.

Consequently, a man or woman who has been married in a Catholic ceremony and subsequently divorced is *not* able to remarry in a Catholic church. However, a priest will marry you if your previous marriage was a civil ceremony and you have then been legally divorced, because your marriage would not have been recognised according to the Catholic faith. You can also remarry in church if your former spouse is no longer living. If one of the couple who are to be married was previously married in a church of another denomination or with a civil ceremony only, you should consult your priest.

In certain circumstances, the Church does allow for an annulment of a marriage, but it is a lengthy and extremely difficult process to have a previous marriage declared null and void, and takes a considerable time to obtain. Again, you will need to meet with your priest to discuss your situation and for more details about what is involved in this procedure.

Jewish weddings

The Chief Rabbi in the UK, Dr Jonathan Sacks, made this wise comment about his own marriage: 'I think we understood that love means giving, not taking, that marriage is the poetry of everyday life.'

According to the Board of Deputies, marriages within the Jewish community are continuing to decline. The total number of synagogue marriages in the UK in the year 2000 was 907, a sharp decrease of 11 per cent from 1999. Meanwhile, the number of mixed-faith couples, in which one of the partners is Jewish, marrying in a registrar's office is on the increase.

Confusion often arises about whether there are differences between Orthodox, Reform, or Liberal Jewish weddings, and depending on where you first got married and what your plan is this time, you will need to consult with your own rabbi about your status. If you want a synagogue wedding this time, remember a secular divorce does not count if either the prospective bride or groom was previously married in a synagogue.

There are ways round this but it is not easy, for while Judaism reluctantly recognises the need for divorce 'in the proper context' it is extremely complicated to bring about. For a Jewish couple to be divorced they must obtain a '*get*' – a document recognised by Jewish law as separating 'the soul of the man and woman'.

If a Jewish woman wants to remarry, she will need informed advice about how to go about obtaining a *get* since the *get* must be applied for by the man and given to the woman. If an ex-husband refuses to cooperate and give his wife a religious divorce, a Jewish woman can be left in the dreadful position of having obtained a civil divorce but still not free to remarry in synagogue. The thinking behind this is that there should be no marriage without consent, and therefore no divorce without consent. Should a man who was married in a synagogue wish to remarry in synagogue, a *get* will be required in order to show, in the interests of sexual equality today, that he has freed his former wife from the first marriage.

A traditional Jewish wedding is a warm and joyous affair, from the joining of the two families under the *chuppah* (canopy) to the bridegroom stamping on and breaking a wine glass with the congregation joining in a chorus of '*Mazeltov!*' ('Good luck!'). There are several explanations for this last tradition: one is that even in the midst of personal happiness and celebration there should be acknowledgement of sadness in the world. Another is that it is a reminder of the destruction of the Temple. The one I prefer is that the act of breaking the wine glass reminds us all of the fragility of personal relationships and is there to ensure that the bride and groom remember to take good care of their marriage.

Non-conformist weddings

If you were married in a church and have been divorced, prior to 2002 you were more likely to find a Non-conformist minister willing to marry you than a Church of England vicar. Church of Scotland, Methodist, Baptist or United Reformed ministers will, at times, allow someone to remarry after a divorce. The Methodist minister who spoke with me explained that any couple talking to him should be prepared to discuss what went wrong before, and to look at what has been learned from the past.

Although there is a 'right to be married', if a minister has a crisis of conscience for any reason, the couple may well be passed on to another minister who is prepared to marry them. So do not take anything for granted, as a decision will depend on individual circumstances.

To remarry in church you may well have to show real conviction that you are serious about a new start and that being married in church again is most important to you. So, a word of caution, make sure that you are ready to explain just why you or your partner want a second wedding to take place in church. Then make an appointment to discuss your situation with the minister in the church of your choice.

Unitarian Church weddings

Unitarians do not view vows of marriage as a sacrament. Thus a joining of two people in a marriage service is not seen as 'ordained by God' but as a decision made by two people.

This Church welcomes flexibility of thought and beliefs, and a minister will work with a couple who wish to marry, in order to understand their needs and wishes. The prospective bride and groom will be helped to decide the form of language used in the ceremony, and the minister will be guided by the requirements of the couple in relation to readings, music and vows. He will need to be satisfied that the couple have thought seriously about marriage, and that they wish to celebrate in a spiritual context. A growing number of people who have been divorced, but who wish to remarry in church for spiritual reasons, are turning to this church, where they feel they are welcome.

Unitarians will perform marriage ceremonies for people

of mixed faiths, and a Unitarian wedding might include readings from the Koran or the Bible.

Unitarian weddings in England and Wales must take place during daylight in a building registered for public worship and for solemnisation of weddings. In Scotland the wedding can be at any hour and in virtually any location, including the great outdoors. Religious ceremonies of blessing following a civil marriage may take place at any suitable location, including the garden of your own home. You do not need to be a regular member of the Unitarian Church to be able to talk to them about a wedding ceremony or a religious blessing of a civil marriage ceremony.

> Pablo: 'Oh, the relief at finding a minister prepared to talk to us. Do tell people about this church.'

For more information see www.unitarian.org.uk or email ga@unitarian.org.uk.

A Humanist wedding

Contact the British Humanist Society (www.humanism. org.uk) if you want to know more about planning a Humanist ceremony. If this is what you and your partner are considering, it is as well to remember that a Humanist wedding is not legally recognised in the UK, so a civil ceremony preceding the Humanist service is necessary.

Among the helpful information provided by the society is

a very important piece of advice: remember that at the *civil* ceremony you do not need to exchange rings and that you only need to have two witnesses present. This enables many couples to count their marriage from the time of their Humanist wedding, treating the civil ceremony simply as a formal occasion to give them legal married status. (This has wider implications since once the legal requirement is out of the way you are free to plan your wedding ceremony in any way you want to.)

> Roger: 'We had a very low-key civil ceremony the day before our wedding. We considered the registrar's bit just as the business part. Our wedding was quite another thing.'

An experienced Humanist celebrant will help you to prepare for your wedding, and will meet up with you well before the day, and be able to offer advice on music and readings. The chosen pieces will be non-religious. Some couples told me that they devised a very special, personal, wedding service written by themselves 'from the heart', and it is possible to invite a friend or relative to take part – a good way of involving others in your special ceremony. The most important part of the ceremony is when you state your promises to each other: by choosing or writing your own passages you will be able to say exactly what you want to convey.

Jess told me that she felt her second wedding was the most beautiful occasion she had ever been too. They chose an outdoor setting, at dusk, with music and readings which meant a great deal to Jess and her new husband. She said that even her parents, who were very much against a second wedding at all, were overcome by the beauty of it.

Luke: 'My wife and I began to get second wedding blues when trying to plan a meaningful ceremony. We had both been married before, and we couldn't believe the hassle we ran into with us both coming from different religious backgrounds. People were so unhelpful. The Humanist belief in the right to freedom of choice, and belief in "doing as you would be done by" felt so right. Thank goodness we found them just in time. We had a lovely ceremony which meant so much to us both.'

The British Humanist Association is a registered charity, and in these times where there seems to be a growing need for non-religious ceremonies, many couples are finding this ceremony is just what they are looking for. I can well understand what a great relief this is for many couples who find themselves out in the cold when trying to plan a second wedding day.

Quaker weddings

A Quaker wedding is probably the most simple ceremony of all. It takes place in a Quaker Meeting House. If you want to marry for a second time and you are a Quaker, you must consult at the monthly meeting so that the members can decide whether or not to give permission for the marriage to take place. If all is well, there will be a registering officer (Quaker's have their own registrars) and the couple will make a commitment to each other in the presence of God and their family and friends. They will ask God's blessing on their life-time union.

It is most likely the couple will be dressed quite simply. The wedding ceremony will be very informal as there will be no priest or minister leading the service, and the couple will sign the Quaker wedding certificate which records their promises. The witnesses and all those present will also sign, and then the registering officer will read out the whole certificate. The civil register will also be signed. If a divorced person wants to remarry, the registering officer will need to know that he or she is legally free to do so.

Pagan weddings

When I first had an enquiry from a couple wanting to know more about a Pagan wedding, I must confess I was rather thrown for answers.

Phil: 'I want a very simple second wedding. What about jumping over the broomstick – is that a Pagan kind of wedding? Please advise.'

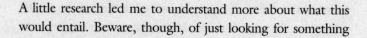

A little research led me to understand more about what this would entail. Beware, though, of just looking for something different or novel as Pagan weddings are taken by some people very seriously indeed. A wedding can be as simple as a couple taking their vows before the gods and human witnesses of your choice. You can do that anywhere, anytime. The important thing is that you formally make promises to each other before witnesses who can hold you accountable to them. (But a word of caution again, this verbal agreement will not be legally binding: to fulfil legal requirements a ceremony in the UK must be performed in premises licensed for weddings.)

Phil is correct in thinking that a custom in Pagan weddings is to jump over the broom, a broom which has been used 'to sweep away all negative vibrations'. I learned, too, that many customs we associate with marriage today may owe their roots to Pagan customs, such as throwing the garter or the bouquet, the groom not being allowed to see the bride beforehand, and even the throwing of rice. Couples speak to each other of their commitment, and sometimes their wrists are tied together (also called handfasting). To complicate matters slightly, I learned that handfasting is the marriage rite used by many non-Pagans. I like the fact that the promises are made 'for a year and a day, renewable so long as love shall last'. Perhaps that keeps people on their toes instead of letting love slip away as so many couples sadly do over time.

Pagan ceremonies are traditionally held out of doors and this seems to link up with one of the oldest and universal traditions – a belief in the power of nature. Often a simple ceremony, written by the couple themselves, will consist of a statement of beliefs, but it is possible to find a priest or priestess to conduct a slightly more formal service.

If you want to be married at an ancient site, English

Heritage or the National Trust should be consulted as permission will be needed. If the venue you select is going to be hard for guests to find, be sure to provide a good map. Make sure your clothes are robust enough if you have to walk across fields, and watch out for the weather – especially in the UK! Hopefully the place you select will have room to erect a tent or marquee which will be a blessing for your guests, especially the older members.

Gay and lesbian weddings

Same-sex weddings are not yet recognised by law in the UK, and the dispute rages within the Anglican Church about performing blessings for same sex unions, but an increasing number of gay men and women want to make a declaration of their commitment to each other in public. Therefore affirmation ceremonies, or commitment ceremonies, are now becoming popular.

The Pink Triangle Trust's affirmation ceremony of love and commitment is often taken as a guideline; it is a quite simple affair, often with only a few close friends and family present. The PTT is a charitable trust set up in 1992 and the main activities of the Trust are the arrangement of affirmation ceremonies. The Trust can arrange a secular Humanist ceremony for same-sex couples at a reasonable cost in most parts of the UK. The ceremony is conducted by a friendly, experienced celebrant who will want to visit the couple in advance to discuss the details. The PTT ceremony brochure can be obtained by phoning 01926 85850, or by e-mail from ceremonies@pinktriangle.org.uk.

Angie: 'Well, human rights and all that. We wanted, and planned, a civil union ceremony and all our friends loved the ceremony and the party.'

Robert: 'We had both had a traditional heterosexual wedding in the past – what a farce! I knew at the time that it was all wrong, but that is what you did in those days. This time we had a truly wonderful commitment ceremony, and it was gay in every sense of the word. I never dreamed I would find such happiness.'

Bob: 'My first wedding was a sham, really, but I went through the motions. This time my affirmation ceremony with Rick was a wonderful, meaningful experience. What a difference! I felt I had truly found peace and love.'

It is also possible to have your relationship blessed by an ordained minister. The choice is getting wider as you can see by visiting the website www.pinktriangle.org.uk.

There are some countries where civil (or registered) partnerships give limited marriage rights to lesbian and gay couples. The Foreign and Commonwealth Office (telephone 0207 270 1500) will give further information about embassies in countries outside the UK.

The Lesbian and Gay Christian Movement (www.lgcm.org.uk) will also give guidelines on how to arrange a service of blessing.

The Greater London Partnerships Register was set up in September 2001 by the Greater London Authority. It enables couples, both same-sex and heterosexual, to register formally their partnership's status where one partner is a London resident. The registration does not automatically confer legal rights as marriage does, but as I was advised by the secretary of the PTT, it is a step towards avoiding problems arising over housing, taxation, inheritance rights and family law. It may also be used as additional evidence in any dispute or civil action that might arise. If you want more information about the partnership contact: www.london. gov.uk/approot/mayor/partnerships/index.jsp.

The registration is held at GLA premises. A certificate of registration is provided and a ceremony with invited guests can be conducted afterwards by the PTT among others. Information can be obtained by phoning the GLA on 020 7983 4458 or e-mailing lpr@london.gov.uk.

Hostile reactions to mixed-faith weddings

'All you need is love', sang the Beatles in the sixties, and we have all been singing along ever since. But regrettably this message isn't always how things are. Perhaps this is most evident when a couple who come from different religious backgrounds want to plan a wedding. This is where decisions about where a marriage will be performed, often a family issue, can soon grow into a fireball. It is usually because the couple come from completely different religions. What may also be on the cards is where either one of the couple declares that religion has no importance to them, while the other takes religion very seriously. So any pair are well advised to talk this through right at the beginning. To wait may mean that one of them finds him or herself bewildered when the other begins to steam ahead and make plans for a religious or non-religious ceremony.

Couples can find, sometimes much to their surprise, that parents and grandparents often mind very much indeed if their child – no matter what age! – is planning to marry someone from a different religion. Perhaps there is no other situation which can bring about so much shouting and so many tears and even threats of 'You are killing your mother/father/grandparents.' This can be a particularly difficult time if you are having to battle with family disappointment and even downright prejudice about your choice of life partner.

And yet in society today, people of all faiths and cultures mix together and it is not surprising that an increasing number of couples find themselves facing a dilemma they had not thought would be an issue. Some may have anticipated parental disapproval about a remarriage, but are taken completely by surprise by the strength of the expression of religious feelings.

Maggie wrote to tell me: 'I had no idea that my parents would be so against my marriage to someone of a different religion. I can't believe this is happening to us. I thought they might fuss because my fiancé has been married before, but not because he is RC.' Maggie and her fiancé felt they had no option but to go for a civil ceremony – without the blessing or attendance of either set of parents. 'We are both still in shock about it all,' said Maggie.

If only we'd known …

'Oh the hypocrisy. My dad never even goes to church,
but he went ballistic when I said we were having a
civil wedding. Jeremy has been married before and is
Jewish, and I thought that *was going to be the*
problem with my family. But no, the fact that we
couldn't be married in our local church because of
Jeremy's divorce brought about the most terrible
family rows. We nearly split up about it, but we are
both good people even though Dad tried to make out
we were wicked. He didn't come to our wedding.'

Reggie, who is Jewish, was forced into an impasse: 'My parents took an unbelievably impossible stand and before we could discuss options declared they would not be at the wedding. I was so angry I immediately agreed to marry in a church, which was the wish of my future wife anyway.'

'My mother wept when I told her I was marrying a non-Jew. "What about the children? What about the children?" She gave no thought to the fact that I am in my late forties and I have had a hysterectomy. So what children?' Eliza told me that she thought what was really on her mother's mind was that both her brothers had married 'out' and none of her grandchildren were being brought up in the Jewish faith.

If only we'd known …

'My grandmother came straight out and told me that there were two bad omens surrounding my forthcoming marriage. One, that I was marrying a divorced man with children, and two, that we had different religious backgrounds. She said, "This marriage of yours is doomed to fail. Don't say I didn't warn you." I cried for a week.'

It can come as a surprise, too, that friends whom you thought would be understanding express their doubts about the wisdom of an interfaith marriage. At its worst, the disagreements can cause a rift between the intended couple themselves and family and friends. Some couples told me they were met with a barrage of criticism and comments such as: 'Do you realise what you are doing to your parents?', 'Are you prepared for some of the family to stop seeing you?', 'Don't give me that rubbish about letting your future children choose their own religion, it will be too late' and 'There is a price to be paid for inter-faith marriages. The cost is very high.'

But from Cyril: 'I cannot believe this. We have both been divorced and are not young, and yet both sets of parents have "told us off" because we want to marry. Until we announced our engagement neither of us had even *thought* about the religious differences.'

Judith was another one who was not happy with the solution: 'I was married in a synagogue the first time, and the marriage was a disaster. This time I would like to please my future husband who has not been married before. However, I cannot feel right about marrying in a church and so we have decided on a register office. We are sad that in our forties we have ended up distressing both lots of parents.'

Harry: 'We are both Christians in the active sense, but neither of our churches would marry us. We come from opposite ends of the evangelical church scene – circles which never come anywhere close to each other. The word bargepole comes to mind. It is impossible and we were on the brink of splitting up because it was all becoming so ridiculous.'

Here is a typical e-mail from among the many I receive on the difficulties surrounding mixed faith marriages: 'Assist us please. We want to marry. We have religious, cultural and geographical differences, oh, and language, too, of course. What problems should we look out for?'

Such a couple need to realise that there will be a good chance of encountering (as we have already seen) disapproval from parents and friends. How will they feel about this? Are they both prepared to cope with possible alienation from one side of the family? Are they prepared for one or the other to let go of some traditions and national celebrations? To accept that any children may come up against a language barrier with one set of grandparents? To move to another country? If you are in such a situation are you prepared for devastating consequences of this kind?

If there are children to be considered, now or in the future, it is imperative that there is an early discussion about how they will be brought up and taught. It may seem light-years away, and something that 'won't bother us', but you will be surprised how time flies: suddenly you will be faced by the realisation that your children are going to be taught to disregard something you hold dear. Discuss this in advance! It is easier to talk about a possible scenario early on rather than to wait until a decision must be made and the accusations fly with 'You never said …' or 'I thought we agreed …' So do take care here.

It is a very sad thing when families are divided by religious or cultural differences. I found that most couples faced with difficulties over a mixed marriage and by the distress of differing family views had to settle for a civil wedding, very often after many tears had been shed along the way.

Some couples decide to organise a blessing ceremony afterwards. If this is what you would like, then speak to a minister, priest, rabbi or other officiating dignitary. Hopefully, you will find a sympathetic ear and even ministers from different faiths who are prepared to work together.

And yet, even this compromise distresses some families. 'I can't believe my daughter thought this would satisfy us. I think it is a dilution of all religions,' said Jim.

One excellent website is www.foreignwives.com which provides a forum for women to 'let off steam' and to share their experiences of living in a foreign country.

Of course, many mixed faith or cross cultural marriages are hugely successful. But think through all the implications, and above all discuss them together in advance!

A final word from Daniel: 'We thought we were up against it because of our different religious backgrounds. We talked and talked, and then decided that two faiths were better than none. We have been happily married for over twenty years. You need to be sensitive and respectful of each other's beliefs.' Daniel's example will, I am sure, be a source of comfort for many couples.

If only we'd known ...

'On our wedding night, we sighed with relief that it was all over. Somehow on the way we had both alienated our parents because of different religions. And both our daughters had refused to come to the wedding for their own reasons. Don't let anyone tell you that getting married a second time is easy. Not with family and especially not with children around.'

6

The reception

'The guests are met, the feast is set
Mays't hear the merry din.
The wedding guest he beat his breast,
For he heard the loud bassoon.'
SAMUEL TAYLOR COLERIDGE,
The Rime of the Ancient Mariner

Why not celebrate?

Many couples who marry for a second time ponder over whether they really want a reception. Of course, it is not an essential part of a wedding, but it is pleasant to celebrate. And it is one more element at a second wedding that serves to bond everyone together and often among the most memorable parts of the day, especially if there are good speeches (more about this later!).

I have heard from couples who opted for a quiet meal after a short ceremony, and most of them later regretted it. So why not push the boat out? It does not have to cost an arm and a leg. Not everyone has to spend a fortune like the ex-Beatle Paul McCartney. At his second wedding the guests danced to five bands and enjoyed a 'feast of curries laid out in an Indian-themed marquee draped with Indian silk and velvet cushions'.

If only we'd known ...

*'We had both been married before so we didn't
celebrate at all. Later we heard from friends
and family how hurt they felt to be left out of
our wedding day.'*

A reception at home

There are families who will not consider having a wedding
reception anywhere else but at home. And you don't need a
huge house to be able to do this in style. Of course, if there
is space for a marquee all well and good, there will be more
room and you will not be such a hostage to fortune with the
weather. You don't necessarily have to go so far as hiring an
expensive marquee, an awning or tent rigged up in the
garden will often do just as well.

But remember what this day is all about: it is for those
close to you, who care about you, to come and wish you
well. Nobody really *needs* an expensively catered banquet,
and one bride told me that they included in their invitations
a short request: in lieu of a gift please bring a salad or side-
dish to share at the potluck reception immediately following
the ceremony. She went on to tell me that as they had both
come into this, their second marriage, at totally different

points in their lives, they decided to be sensible about costs. 'Reality bites if you spend too much on the wedding,' this bride told me.

The first thing to decide upon is what kind of reception you would like. An informal 'anything goes' party? A reception which is as elegant as possible? A barbecue where it is all hands on deck? A drinks party with nibbles? If you decide to hire a local hall, find out right at the beginning whether you will need any special licences for music and alcohol.

Other wedding couples told me of various ways to provide a spread without breaking the bank. With freezers and microwaves it is now possible for the wedding couple themselves – with plenty of preparation beforehand – to feed the family and friends who come to party with them. This is often a way for second wedding couples to proceed.

If only we'd known …

'People promised to help, but then didn't deliver! So, an hour before my own wedding I was at the supermarket.'

If you are to have your reception in your own home, and you plan to do without a caterer, make sure you ask in advance for plenty of help on the day. You can't be the bride *and* the hostess worrying if the sausages have been cooked. Get a friend to take over handling the drinks, and another to keep an eye on the refreshments. If you want to have music, ask a friend to look after organising this (and make sure your preferences are top of the list!). Part of the fun of a home-grown wedding reception is that everybody does join in, and you will find that people like to be involved. Have a good friend on 'standby' who can dash off to the shops if you run out of any essentials. But remember, it is *your* wedding celebration, and you are there to enjoy yourself!

If you are going for a grander affair at home (or the home of a relative or 'dear' friend!) be realistic about your plans. Ask the caterer for advice about how many people will be comfortable, and whether a stand-up buffet or a sit-down meal is best. And take their advice.

Nobody really enjoys a wedding where the world and his wife have been invited and there is nowhere to sit down. Be sure your guests are comfortable, even if it means moving out most of the furniture to make extra space. Also, remember that anything of value which might get broken or damaged should be hidden away. That way, you can relax. One caterer I spoke to said that when the hired tables and chairs are delivered, he takes away some of the furniture from the house and leaves it in his van until the party is over.

Remember, too, to check with the caterers how they will

keep food hot and drinks cold. Make certain that you know exactly what they will provide, discuss the menu in the finest detail and again leave nothing to chance. Depending on the time of day that you are getting married you can decide whether you are providing a lunch or tea or an evening 'cocktail party' style of reception. Or you may even choose to marry at midnight! This is what film star Julia Roberts did for her second wedding, and it opens up all kinds of possibilities.

It is as well to get estimates for different meals as the cost may be one of the main factors in helping you decide what to choose. It is very easy to get carried away by selecting and including a 'few' extras, so keep an eye on the budget you agreed on. And wherever you entertain your guests with a meal, remember the vegetarian option. This is becoming more and more popular these days as anyone who has entertained a number of people will tell you.

Will there be room for guests to park? If there are parking restrictions around your house have a word with the parking authorities – you should find they will be receptive and make special arrangements for the hours of your wedding reception. Or they may not! So do the kind thing for your guests and check this out, and even include some reference to this with the invitation you send out.

A reception at home can be a wonderful way to celebrate a wedding in a relaxed and intimate atmosphere, but your heart must be in it, and you will be well advised not only to get as many helpers as you can before and during the day itself, but also with the clearing up the day after.

If only we'd known ...

*'As we had lived together for a year, we decided to
hold the party in our own home after the wedding.
Big mistake. I found it hard to relax, we had
forgotten to send the cat and dogs away, and worst of
all we saw our new furniture and carpets come in for
a hammering. How I wished that for this wedding I
had had a mother-of-the-bride bossing everyone
around. I wept with exhaustion when everybody left.'*

I should just add that several second-time brides who
organised their own wedding receptions said to me that it
was only then that they realised how much work their
mothers had put into planning and organising their first
wedding, something which at the time they took for
granted.

A hotel reception

Whether or not your wedding has been celebrated at a hotel
licensed to perform marriages – and everything under one
roof certainly cuts down on the organisation – many couples
choose to have the reception in a hotel. If this is what you
decide, then be sure to visit several places and study them
with a very beady eye. Save valuable time by checking first

by telephone to make sure they have a space available for your proposed date. Also, that they have a licence to perform marriages.

I went to one hotel recently which advertised a package deal for weddings. I saw the room where the service could take place, but unfortunately at times this doubled as a dining room, and the smell of the previous day's food was most unappealing.

In another I found that if it was raining the bridal party would have to go down the backstairs of the hotel, past the kitchen and up two flights of stairs to arrive at the room designated for marriages. When we were shown the suite there was no mention of this, only a pretty patio entrance. So examine any venue with the utmost care.

Another couple told me of their anguish when they discovered that the room provided for the reception was not the room they had been shown previously, but one with a huge billiard table in the centre.

This couple contacted me to urge any couples who are marrying to check and check again the facilities and services they are booking. Unscrupulous people bank on the couple not wanting to make a fuss on 'the day', so do go over details in good time, and then once more for luck! This goes for menus, cars, flowers, music, cakes and caterers. Don't take anything on trust or in a spirit of goodwill.

Make certain you get *all* agreements in writing too, with as much detail as possible. It is no good saying later, 'Oh, I thought you meant' or 'We thought you would provide ...' The professionals who provide the services are not mind-readers, so be precise about what you want. Spell out the whole shebang in exact detail every step of the way.

If only we'd known ...

'If you have a guest book, ask someone to stand by it and advise guests where to sign. We didn't, and we ended up with several unplanned – and sometimes unsuitable – comments and drawings by children and adults.'

It is never too soon to start looking as the most attractive sites get booked up long in advance. Don't just go on a recommendation – make up your own mind. Ask, too, if another wedding is planned for the same day, and whether the hotel can cope with this. Don't be shy at asking all sorts of questions. If you are also to be married in the hotel, how will the transition from the ceremony to the reception be handled? Will it be private enough, or will other hotel guests get caught in with your party? Will there be a room for you to change your clothes? Is there enough parking space? If you want specific touches, ask if you are allowed to have candles, balloons or confetti. Is there a time you have to be 'out' by, and if not will there be overtime for the staff? Will there be sufficient chairs? Will the tables be the right size for the number of people placed at them? Is there enough space between them for the staff to get around? Are the glasses and cutlery of the right quality? The list is endless.

If only we'd known ...

'A room in a pub was booked. At the last moment we were told we couldn't put up our decorations until after closing time at 11 p.m. The wedding was quite early next morning, so we were a very tired wedding party!'

Adam: 'We provided a solution when we found that there were going to be thirty children at the wedding reception. What we did was this – we all mingled and had drinks and photographs and then when it was time to eat the adults went into the main room for a grand meal, and the kids went into a tent in the garden – where there was someone disguised as a clown to supervise them – for burgers, pizza and chips. It might not have been the healthiest meal, but it bought us all some pleasant grown-up time.'

Try to get a feel of the place, and think about whether you

would all be happy and relaxed there. If it is a hotel, have a meal there to help you to decide about the quality and the presentation of the food. If you are going to decorate a room you have hired check what time you can begin your preparation.

Music is a very personal choice, so whether booking a quartet, a harp, band or DJ don't just take a friend's word for it. Ask around. Consider getting music school students to provide the music for your reception. These young people are often excellent musicians and will be happy to play for you, probably at a much lower fee than you might expect. Be sure you are able to listen to them before you make a firm commitment. Talk over how long they will play for and what their repertoire will be. I heard from Peter that at his father's second wedding – the couple were both in their late seventies – the band began to play and sing, 'We've got all the time in the world.' Within minutes, all the guests were in tears. So do take care.

If you are concerned about sticking to your budget, keep in mind that the cheapest services on offer are not always the bargain they claim to be, so look carefully for any hidden extras.

When Kathy went to collect the flowers for her table decorations she found they were not the carefully selected colours which had been specifically matched with the colour scheme for the bridesmaids' dresses. Fortunately, Kathy still had the sample of ribbon she had shown the florist and which he had agreed to match. So she was on firmer ground to complain than she would have been if she had described from memory the shade she wanted.

Two last things which are all too often forgotten about: enquire about insurance, in case a guest gets injured, and it is as well to check out and review the cancellation policy for all the professional services you are involved with. You never know if, for example, illness will strike.

Do all your planning well in advance, and have the party of your lives. Whether you opt for a home celebration, a hotel reception or a 'bit of a do' in a pub, make the most of it. The secret is to check and check again beforehand, and then on the day you should be able to rest assured that you are in safe professional hands. You can then just relax and enjoy yourselves, which is as it should be.

Of course, if you are a popstar and you plan to be whisked away from the reception, choose a setting which has a helipad. A very dramatic exit for any bridal couple!

Destination weddings

If only we'd known ...

*'Oh! If only we had known how complicated it is to
get sixteen people to and from a wedding in the heart
of France! Two were ill, one lost her passport and cash,
and my brother went off in a huff.'*

If you are looking for a wedding with a difference, there is a lot to be said for getting right away by going off to the place of your dreams. Many second-time around couples told me they opted for a 'getaway' wedding. There were too many memories around and about, and the thought of a totally different setting had a special appeal to them. Part of the attraction is that it is carefree and spontaneous, but actually it does need quite a bit of forethought and planning.

'We went back to Greece,' said Dominic. 'We had a simple but wonderful wedding in the Mayor's office, and a feast under the stars with our friends.' He had to pay for advertising their 'intent to marry' in the local press, but that 'didn't break the bank'. 'We would have liked to have been married in the church there, but neither of us was Greek Orthodox or Catholic,' he added, rather wistfully.

For his second wedding, Sir Paul McCartney opted for a location 'away from it all', a romantic seventeenth-century castle. Although in this case, he and Heather Mills, his bride-to-be, took with them a plane-load of guests ... and the world's press! Other brides marrying for a second time may like to note that Ms Mills was able to marry at the church at Castle Leslie under Church of Ireland rules. A local priest conducted the ceremony.

There are plenty of 'destination wedding' ideas available; most travel agents will come up with suggestions and a package deal for you. You will find offers with a variety of options, including exchanging your vows in one exotic resort and celebrating your honeymoon in another. Groups of friends or family can be catered for too. You should make sure that in addition to your standard holiday insurance you can purchase extra cover for weddings.

If only we'd known ...

*'Did you know that the final papers about a divorce
do not always come through as quickly as you
anticipate. Beware! There was a slip-up with my
final decree, and as we had booked the wedding and
reception we had to skip the wedding and go to the
reception with smiles on our faces as if we had just
been married! So, my advice to any couple: make sure
there is time for everything to be in order.'*

You will find that if you want to be married abroad you
need to give plenty of notice so as to get all the paperwork
done in time. You may be asked to send a sworn declaration
or affidavits in advance, as some countries demand a
'Certificate of No Impediment'. This is a declaration that
the couple wishing to marry are indeed free to do so. The
Statutory Declaration is a written statement sworn to be
true in front of a solicitor, and you should have this
document translated into the language of the country where
you want to marry.

Make sure in good time that you have on hand any
documents you will need, such as your divorce papers, birth
certificate and, if appropriate, the death certificate of a
spouse. Find out, too, if there are restrictions about
residency beforehand: often, depending on your destination,
there is a requirement for the couple to be resident for a

minimum number of working days before the ceremony can take place. Ask if you will have to pay extra for the marriage licence once you reach your destination.

You will have to take quite a lot of the arrangements on trust if you go for a 'deal', so you may prefer to make all the arrangements yourself. The Internet facilitates this, but check, and make sure again, that there are no additional formal requirements you need to have sorted before you can marry. To get an idea of the destinations on offer visit www.world-weddings.net. There are other sites which offer the full works, even providing an interpreter for the wedding ceremony and assistance with the paperwork required. Excellent sites for any couple wanting to marry in Italy are www.weddings inItaly.com and www.venice-weddings.com which are full of information covering important details you may not know, such as that civil and Roman Catholic weddings cannot take place outdoors, yet Protestant weddings can.

Those who can come along with you will no doubt enter into the fun of it all, but opinions are divided about who should pay for the additional expenses of travelling and accommodation. So think this very important issue through right at the beginning. Remember that with some destinations the actual date of the wedding ceremony cannot be confirmed until you arrive, so you need to bear this in mind if you are taking guests along with you.

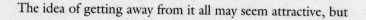

The idea of getting away from it all may seem attractive, but it will require organisation down to the smallest detail. And, if this is your choice, take into account that it is unlikely that everyone who would like to be present will be able to make it. Maybe this is what you have in mind, and what has prompted you to think of 'getting away'!

Abigail: 'We all went to Florida for our wedding. It was great. After the ceremony and lovely reception my sister took our kids to another hotel to give us some privacy. Watch out for hidden extras and "optional touches". The cost of these can mount up, but we had a wonderful time.'

If only we'd known …

'I woke up on my wedding day with a terrible stomach-ache. I thought it was stress because my ex was kicking up such a storm. I went to my second wedding almost doubled up and had to go from the service to the hospital. An appendix of all things. So that is where I spent my honeymoon.'

Maggie sent me a frantic e-mail to say that her daughter was getting married in Las Vegas. It was a second wedding for both her and her partner, and they are both 'in their fifties'. Maggie's dilemma was how to tell family and friends that they were welcome to the wedding and reception but would have to pay for their own accommodation and flights. This is another example of a family – in this case the mother of the bride – worrying about what to tell people. Fear of what 'people will think' lurks behind this. I replied that I felt the only way was to be upfront and direct with everyone. After all, the people they invited would all be close to the family, and I felt a telephone call saying just what Maggie said to me, would make things clear.

It is perfectly permissible to telephone, or write, to say that the couple would love to have you at the wedding, but they realise that the cost of the flight and accommodation might mean that you can't make it. If the answer comes back 'We're coming', then a more formal invitation can be sent giving the details. I think it is reasonable to assume that guests will not expect all their costs to be met, but leave nothing to chance, and spell out the details. If the wedding is going to involve considerable travel plans, guests will need plenty of notice about the date.

Jim and Elaine thought it unlikely that many of their family or friends would be able to come with them to Jamaica. They solved the problem in this way: 'We sent out formal invitations, and a handwritten note to say that we would also have a party on our return for everyone to celebrate our marriage. And it seemed to work, nobody got upset.'

Did you know you can still marry at Gretna Green? This location dates back to 1710 where runaway couples from England would get married as soon as they crossed into

Scotland. A legal, Christian service, or a civil marriage, can be arranged for you in a setting with all the original features of the period. Visit www.gretnaweddings.com for all the information you need about a wedding 'over the anvil at the Gretna Green Blacksmith's Hall'. However, you will find that although the romantic idea of just running off to Scotland and Gretna Green is still an option, it is just like any other wedding where the paperwork is concerned. Forms M10 (Marriage Notice – Scotland) must be completed and returned by both the prospective bride and groom up to three months but no later than fifteen days before the wedding – together with a cheque. Other required documents are also needed in good time.

If only we'd known ...

'We had an assembly-line wedding in Japan. It was stress free, but there was no originality and I hated it. It was a wedding for the guests not the couple. We made up for it with a lovely honeymoon though.'

Briony had a different kind of worry: 'Do you call ours a destination wedding? I am getting married abroad because that is what my husband-to-be's family want. I won't know anyone there. But I have asked that the ceremony be translated.' I am not sure that this is a destination wedding in the usual sense, but a lot of the same rules apply, such as getting all the necessary documents.

Take care if you plan a wedding miles away from home, that you don't make friends and family anxious about what is expected of them. You may think you have spelt out what you want, but people may still be troubled about 'What is the right thing to do?', especially if they do not want to hurt or upset you both in any way. 'What is the proper etiquette regarding participation and gifts?' asked a worried aunt. 'We can't afford to go but don't like to say so,' said a good friend of the bride and groom. And in another e-mail: 'Please send guidelines for the difficult and uncomfortable situation of a wedding in another country.'

The couples concerned were probably unaware of how perturbed so many people were by their decision to have a 'getaway wedding'. So if this is your choice, make sure you add to your list of things to do, 'Be clear about what is expected from friends and relations and ensure that they have no worries.'

When Toby and Melinda decided to marry they were faced by difficulties in every direction, from ex-spouses, from their children, and from friends and family. Indeed, when it seemed unlikely that Toby would get his divorce as quickly as they hoped, they decided enough was enough. Toby and Melinda took the first flight they could to a warm and romantic spot, and there on the sands at dusk said their vows to each other. Toby told me: 'OK, we are not legally married yet, but we just felt we had to get right away and make our promises to each other. We both felt a lot stronger after that and could come back and sort out everything else. When we do have a civil ceremony it will just be a formality. We will never, never forget our "wedding" in the most beautiful setting in the world, just the two of us, just as it should be.'

Points to remember for a destination wedding:

- You will be responsible for all the documentation required, so check and check again that the information you have is correct.
- Keep in mind that your wedding certificate may not be written in English, so you will need to have it translated.
- Make sure you have adequate insurance, especially if travelling with a group of friends and relatives.
- Look out for guests who have their own concerns about 'What is the right thing to do about a destination wedding?'

Ethnic customs

One of the nicest ideas when planning a wedding or reception is to take into consideration any traditions which reflect the ethnic or cultural backgrounds of the bride or groom. So, for instance, you may care to base part of the menu around a dish from a particular country, and if this is what you want, do make sure that you and the chef are speaking the same cookery language. When Helen married Leroy in Liverpool she wanted to make his family feel at home by asking the hotel to provide a traditional West Indian meal. All was agreed, but on the day the bride was horrified to see how badly the chef had interpreted her instructions. So, if you have a special request, don't take the catering manager's word that 'chef will know'. Take a recipe along, and if the reception is to be held in a hotel, ask for a 'trial meal' beforehand. Any chef keen to show off his skills will agree to this. Meanwhile, Helen's effort to please her future in-laws ended with tears, and later a case in court where she was awarded damages against the hotel.

'How can I combine a traditional wedding with some extra acknowledgment to my Chinese groom?' asked Sara. Red is a traditional colour of good luck for the Chinese since it heralds prosperity. So one suggestion might be that the flowers used for decoration and bouquets should be of this colour, with perhaps bridesmaids with red sashes on their dresses. And why not rice instead of confetti? Another idea, if the venue makes this possible, would be to have fireworks at the end of the wedding, because fireworks are a tradition performed at Chinese weddings to ward off evil spirits and to bring good luck. In fact this would be a wonderful way to end any wedding day.

'The family I am marrying into is Irish – I would like to mark this but don't know where to begin,' was an urgent cry from Brenda. To start with, this would be a good moment to have a word with her future mother-in-law and to ask for her help. It would be seen, I am sure, as a sensitive and tactful move. Perhaps using the shamrock, or a green theme with decorations, might be appreciated, but do ask!

Other people often see things very differently and I have heard of one groom's family who were mortally offended when the bride offered only Guinness to drink at the reception, thinking that was what her in-laws would like. A genuine mistake which had unforseen long-term consequences. So do check it out – even well-meaning surprises can misfire.

If you want some sign of national or cultural tradition at your wedding or reception, then something which will brighten up any wedding is the use of national flags. If you make a feature of this it can be a splendid and very effective idea, and a great reminder of 'home'.

I have heard from black women in both the US and the UK that today many Afro-American men and women are determined to add cultural touches to their weddings, as did Carrie: 'I hated my first wedding, but for my second wedding I am determined to have it the way I want it. I am wearing a head wrap, not the stupid tiara I wore before, and I have persuaded my husband-to-be to wear a white suit. I haven't decided yet if I am going to wear full African dress, but my grandmother is very willing to help me with my clothes for the wedding.'

James told me that he and his bride had decided to walk down the aisle to the sound of drums and other African instruments. 'We are also having African dancers at our reception,' he said. Again, I heard of jumping the broom, and of the lovely custom of inviting all the guests to tie a ribbon on to the broom before the ceremony, so that when the couple finally 'jump the broom' they have all the guests' good wishes attached. James told me that the broom symbolises the fact that all past problems have been swept away. 'We both need to believe this,' said James, 'after the bad time we both had with previous partners.'

'No,' said Bennie, 'jumping the broom is a sign of leaving one family behind and of the couple starting a new home together.' Whatever it does symbolise, it sounds a lovely tradition, and one where the roots of this custom go way back in time.

'I am marrying a man from Pakistan,' said Rachel. 'His mother wants me to have my hands and feet decorated with henna designs. What do you think?' Well, I wondered what Rachel herself thought! It seems that since she was writing to me she must be unsure about whether to agree or not. I think it really depends upon whether it would fit in with the plans being made. If she is unhappy about the idea of henna, perhaps it is time to talk with her future husband and his mother about what she would be happy with – and perhaps find another way of incorporating Pakistani ceremonial customs.

From women marrying in Japan I have heard of lovely ceremonies, often where a kimono and wig are worn. The wig, I am told, looks beautiful, but is heavy to wear. It is the custom there for the bride to change from one kimono to another, and to a bridal gown during the reception. Jasmine told me: 'I wore a white kimono which I rented. This is a usual thing to do, and at the reception I changed into a red celebration kimono. During the last part of the reception I changed into a Western-style white dress.'

There are no end of ways to follow traditions and where there are families from different countries or cultural backgrounds it is a terrific idea to incorporate them in the plans. 'We decided to start our own customs – and have a home-spun wedding. We made all the decorations and dresses, the centre-pieces for the tables, my headdress, the bouquets – the lot. When my sister married the following year, she copied all our ideas. Lovely.'

Theme weddings

Hand-in-hand with culturally or ethnically focused weddings go theme weddings, and again there are some excellent websites to help you make your most romantic dreams come true. Be careful not to distract too much from the meaning of the day. And beware of costs if you are planning to wear exotic or period clothes with decorations to match. You will find that this kind of wedding will need the precision and planning of a stage production. It is not something you can decide upon at the last moment. If your dream has always been for a 'fairy-tale wedding', you may even opt for a Disney Deluxe Intimate Wedding Package. This includes a coordinator, choice of flautist or guitarist for the ceremony and a Disney's Fairy-tale Wedding keepsake and, for the bride, a 'romance tote-bag'!

Marie explained that as she had a 'traditional June wedding' the first time round, she opted for a winter wedding and decided she could make a feature of it by wearing a long velvet gown, with bridesmaids dressed warmly as well. They all carried muffs instead of flowers. She made sure that the church was decked with hundreds of candles which gave a soft and warm glow to the ceremony. 'That took some organising,' said Marie.

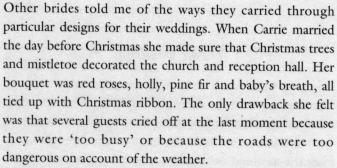

Other brides told me of the ways they carried through particular designs for their weddings. When Carrie married the day before Christmas she made sure that Christmas trees and mistletoe decorated the church and reception hall. Her bouquet was red roses, holly, pine fir and baby's breath, all tied up with Christmas ribbon. The only drawback she felt was that several guests cried off at the last moment because they were 'too busy' or because the roads were too dangerous on account of the weather.

Although Ken and Amy realised that their wedding might have had a touch of the 'Kate Winslets' they opted for a fish-and-chip supper with karaoke. At first, Amy got the feeling that her family thought it was a bit 'naff' but she said the result was the most relaxed wedding imaginable. 'It was certainly unlike any other wedding we had ever been too, including our first weddings. We all laughed so much we cried! A pop star spending two million pounds on a wedding couldn't have had a better time.'

A theme wedding is something which often helps to give a second wedding an original and different slant. For instance, a couple who are mad about horses may choose to have a reception with an equine theme, including decorations consisting of giant horseshoes for good luck, and – if they can run to it – even an ice sculpture of a horse's head. For motor-racing fans I have heard of wedding receptions decorated in a grand-prix style, with names of famous racing drivers instead of table numbers. These individual touches all add to the fun of a second wedding celebration.

> I loved the story of the bride who, without her husband's knowledge, used the colours of his favourite football team and followed this through in the bridesmaids' dresses, in her own bouquet, and in the choice of tablecloths and napkins. No one was left in any doubt about which team he followed. I saw the photographs of what was a charming wedding with a difference, always something to bear in mind for a second wedding, as it was for both this bride and groom.

7

Second wedding dilemmas

'Damn braces. Bless relaxes.'
WILLIAM BLAKE, *The Marriage of Heaven and Hell*

Sex in the twenty-first century

A foreword to *The Art of Marriage* published in the 1950s describes the author's chapters on sex in marriage in this discreet way: 'She is able to speak of the intimate side of marriage with complete frankness; yet with delicacy and good taste.' Nowadays, unlike books published only fifty years ago, books on weddings and marriage ignore the topic completely. Everyone is supposed to 'know it all', so you probably do not expect to be given any pointers about sex in a book about second marriages.

> 'As a second-time bride I am really worried that my intended will compare me to his first wife.'

But the questions come my way: 'We are both marrying for the second time. Of course we have had sex already but it doesn't come up to my memories of making love with my dear husband who died last year. What should I do?', 'I am marrying a woman fifteen years younger than I am. What if she wants sex all the time? What if she wants to be adventurous? I am afraid of the honeymoon. Should I tell her this?', 'I love my husband-to-be dearly, but I don't look like I did when I was a bride the first time around. Should I have any special beauty treatments before our wedding?', 'As a second-time bride I am really worried that my intended will compare me to his first wife. I know they had a good sexual relationship, his sister told me that.'

Perhaps it is on 'the intimate side of marriage' that ex-partners are likely to cast the darkest shadow. Those who have had a bad experience of sex, perhaps associated with violence or betrayal, may be wary about another close sexual relationship. On the other hand, where there are memories of a good sexual pairing there may be anxieties (on both sides) of matching up to expectations. 'Wedding nerves' because of sex may be largely a thing of the past, and explicit knowledge may have replaced the instructions said to be given to Victorian brides to 'lie back and think of England', but all this really does need to be talked about before the wedding day. Don't be embarrassed. You will probably find that your partner will be relieved that you have brought it up, and may have some concerns of his or her own.

Today we are told that 'anything goes', and this alone can petrify a man or woman who may not have had a close sexual relationship for some years. But like any first-time couple, you will learn together what pleases the other. A second-time bride or groom should concentrate on this aspect of making love rather than on the business of comparison. A talk about sex early on should clear the air. (Cover everything, even down to deciding which side of the bed to sleep on, although you may already have sorted that one out.)

It is important to be quite open right from the beginning about the nature of your past relationships, especially so if these are worrying you or you feel they might be causing your partner-to-be anxiety. You may not have lived with anyone for years, but you may have had other kinds of sexual relationships. Why shouldn't you? However, a rule of thumb seems to be that if your intended does not ask you about your 'past', then there is no need to divulge (or boast) about your previous sex life.

Settling down together

You may be anxious about how you or your new partner will adjust to this new life. As I heard from Robert: 'I have had the odd fling over the years since my wife died, but never let anyone move in. Now I am getting married again and find I am suddenly overwhelmed by unease at the thought of how this will affect my new relationship. I am used to doing what I want to when I want to.'

It is not only in the bedroom that there can be anxieties about what it will mean to be married for a second time.

138

Ben told me: 'They say you don't know anybody until you share a bathroom with them. And that is right! Although we had been away for the odd weekend together it wasn't until we married that I saw how untidy Helen is. If I had known before the wedding ...' Happily Ben was only joking, as he went on to urge others – especially if they have not lived with a partner for some time – to give the new relationship space to settle down. 'Just give it time,' said Ben. He wrote to me that he had lived on his own since his divorce ten years previously, and he kept everything in apple-pie order. Helen had other ideas. 'OK,' said Ben, 'I no longer live in the tidiest house on the block, but it certainly is a lot happier place to live in.'

While it takes time for a couple to settle down into a routine and evolve a kind of agreement about who does what, living with a new partner may mean you are in for some surprises. Don't take anything for granted. And certainly beware of remarks such as: 'Oh, I just thought you would take over the garden like Jack did', or 'What! You make gravy from a packet? I have never heard of such a thing! Ellen always made the most tasty gravy.' These remarks may be said unthinkingly, but they hurt just the same.

If it comes as a shock to find that your new partner has ideas that do not fit in with your established routine, just try to be relaxed about it. Do not show too much surprise if you find your new partner likes to get up at five in the morning, or prefers to eat the main meal in the middle of the day, whereas you like to eat late at night. (These are two of the issues which have sent people e-mailing me in a panic on their return from their honeymoons.)

If only we'd known ...

*'I don't think I would have remarried if I had
thought about all the changes I would have to
cope with. Paul says the same. It has
blighted our relationship.'*

The thing is that we all do get a little more set in our ways
as we get older, but remember that this second marriage is a
second chance of happiness, and so ask yourself if these
differences really matter. The answer is for each of you to
'give' a little, so that both of you can contribute to this new
relationship. Once more you are no longer a 'singleton', and
being part of a happy couple is knowing when to make a
stand, and when *not* to.

Together you are building new rituals and customs, and
the more you share with each other the more solid your
relationship becomes. Think of all the exciting things you
will discover about each other over the years. If your partner
has a favourite pastime or hobby, get stuck in there. It is
never too late for you to develop a new interest by having a
door opened on to it by someone who really knows the
subject.

Alice: 'Who would have thought I would ever take to philosophy, but I have. And Edward now comes to the ballet with me.'

Prenuptial agreements

Once upon a time prenuptial agreements were only for the very wealthy. Today they are more common, especially in second and subsequent marriages. As families become more complicated in their make-up, it pays to be more prudent about money matters.

By signing a prenuptial agreement you can ensure that your assets, should there be a divorce, remain your property. Or it may be that, in the event of your death you want to be certain that your property and investments, possibly from an earlier relationship, will pass directly to your children. Such an agreement protects the interests of both parties. But remember, these agreements are not binding in the UK, and only act as a guide to intent. Also, each of you has to consult a different solicitor – one solicitor cannot act for both parties.

If only we'd known ...

'If only I'd known about "prenups" we wouldn't be in the financial mess we are in now that I am remarrying.'

'When I married at seventeen, my then husband took over all the financial matters. Now I have been a widow for nearly twenty years and I am well used to coping with my own money. How do you think my new husband will take this?' With relief, I suspect. It is as well to have a very serious discussion about money matters before your wedding and how you will share the expenses once you are married.

Whereas people used to baulk at the idea of such an unromantic issue – discussing it at all seems to hint at the question 'What if this marriage doesn't work out?' – it is now more acceptable. Even where there are bright expectations of a wonderful future together, women who have been divorced and who perhaps have some property or a cash settlement, want to be sure there will be no problems later on.

'We thought it best to make an agreement. I did have quite a few assets, but my future husband came out of his divorce very badly, with nothing at all,' said Debbie.

If the mention of a prenup agreement does throw up resentment from your intended, then it is as well to have a full discussion about finance *now* so there is no uncertainty later about what is 'yours', 'mine' and 'ours'. Finances for a couple who are both remarrying can be very complicated, especially if one or the other is paying child support. And very often second families can find that money is tight because of earlier commitments. It is as well to talk over whether either of you have other obligations, such as debts or tax owing. Discussions along these lines will also bring out both partners' attitude to money, and that is no bad thing before a wedding. If you have been cohabiting, and signed a cohabitation agreement, this can become the basis for a prenuptial agreement.

This is also a good time to draw up new wills, and to decide whether you need to change the beneficiary on any insurance policies. Be sure to name each child and stepchild – if this applies to you – individually, rather than just 'the children'.

Beware, though, of signing anything too hastily. Such matters are complicated issues, so take your time to talk them through and make sure you both feel comfortable with what is decided. You may like to check for more information on www.freeadvice.com so that you can be prepared before a more formal legal document is drawn up.

> Even with the romantic glow of a wedding about to happen, it is as well to take a moment to consider the 'business' side of a relationship. I hear from too many people who wish they had thought this through years before.

A last point: don't wait until just before the wedding day. This will heighten the tension at a time when most brides and grooms already feel a bit 'edgy'. And a reminder: have you made a new will?

If only we'd known ...

*'I was very upset when Arthur suggested a prenuptial
agreement. It came as a shock. Only later did I
see the wisdom of it.'*

Who will give the bride away?

There are some second-time brides who believe they do
not have to be 'given away' again. Some prefer to be
'escorted' or 'accompanied' down the aisle, and make their
choice accordingly; while others decide to walk by
themselves. And for a second wedding this is one of those
areas where creative thinking can provide you both with a
freer reign.

The father of the bride at a first wedding is a central figure.
As we have seen he is usually the host, and of course he has the
very important job of escorting his daughter down the aisle.
Many a father is only too delighted to repeat this at his
daughter's second wedding, but what if a father refuses to do
it a second time? Don't let this upset the apple cart, because
there is great flexibility about who can play this part. A friend,
one of your children, or perhaps another relative can substitute
for a father who, for his own reasons, doesn't want to be by
your side. There are mothers who are only too willing to step

in if asked, and happy to escort their daughter or even to 'give their daughter away'. So there are plenty of alternatives.

Melinda: 'My best friend is getting married again, and her parents will not come to the wedding. What can we do about giving her away? Will I do?' Yes, of course, a close friend will do very nicely.

These days, when there are so many second marriages, it may not only be the bridal couple who are taking a second chance of happiness: their parents and many of their friends may have been divorced, and quite likely remarried. So a difficult situation can arise over who should give the bride away when there is a father *and* a stepfather who are both willing to walk down the aisle. What is a bride to do in this situation? Annie: 'Both my father and my stepfather assume that they will be giving me away. Oh, the tears that I have shed over this decision.'

This choice is often especially hard if there is a much loved stepfather. Poppy wrote to me: 'Oh, what can I do? Although my future husband has been married before, I have not. My father says unless he is asked to give me away he will not come to the wedding. And yet, my stepfather, who really brought me up, is looking forward to it.'

If only we'd known ...

*'My mother says if I ask my dad to give me away she will
not be able to come to the wedding ceremony. She said he
wasn't there for me as a father when I was growing up,
and has given up the right to a father's privilege. She
wants to be the one to walk me down the aisle.'*

'I'll have both,' cried Elaine. And she did. She came down
the aisle with a father on one arm and a stepdad on the
other, which kept everybody happy.

Another bride said with exasperation: 'Enough! I won't
have anybody. I will walk myself down.' And she did just that.

Unfortunately, there is no perfect solution in such difficult
situations, but I firmly believe that the guiding principle
should be that it is totally out of order for anyone in a
family to 'blackmail' or try to influence a bride in her
choice. It should be acknowledged how difficult it must be
for her already. It is totally out of court for pressure to be
put on her in this sort of way.

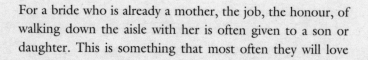

For a bride who is already a mother, the job, the honour, of
walking down the aisle with her is often given to a son or
daughter. This is something that most often they will love

146

to do. It can be a wonderful experience for an older child to escort his or her mother on her wedding day. Indeed, one of the most beautiful weddings I have attended was when the bride was accompanied down the aisle by a son and daughter on either side of her. When the vicar asked, 'Who gives this woman?' there was a delighted chorus of, 'We do'.

There are sometimes worries that this is 'crossing the generation boundary' but I do not see it this way. As more and more second weddings are 'family' weddings, it is a fine way of showing that there is unity in the decision to marry when an older child accepts this honour.

If only we'd known ...

*'My stepdad brought me up from the age of five, yet I
have a father too. I did not want to choose between
them and asked a girlfriend to give me away.
My stepdad and mum thought it a good idea, but my
dad went mad and said he should give me away.
Then my gran said she wouldn't come if dad didn't
give me away. In the end I let him, and thought it
would keep the peace. But I ended up hurting
my mum, stepdad, and dad – because, although
he'd won, he said I had really upset him – and
my gran and grandad, who became ill with the
strain. I wished we had eloped.'*

'Of course I will,' said thirteen-year-old Barry when he was asked if he would like to escort his mother. 'Grandpa did it last time, and now it's up to me.' And he did. No one could have looked prouder than Barry as he walked with his mother down the aisle, followed by his two little sisters in rose-coloured gowns. There was a collective sigh of happiness from the congregation, most of whom knew what an unhappy time this family had experienced over the past years. This day was truly a fresh start for them.

Pity Eliza: she has three adult sons and her concern is which son should walk her down the aisle. 'My middle son,' she queried, 'because he hasn't ever had the attention given to an older or younger brother? Or my eldest, because he is the eldest? Or my "baby"?' Eventually it was decided by consensus that sons number one and two would escort their mother, and the youngest would stand at the altar to be part of the group which would include the groom and his father, who was the best man.

Donna was married in a small wedding chapel. There were only ten people there, including the bridal couple, and no reception had been organised. Donna e-mailed me: 'I hadn't thought of anyone giving me away until the preacher asked. My son stepped forward to do the honours, and it meant the world to me that he put aside his personal feelings to make sure I was happy. For that I will always be grateful.'

If, sadly, the father of the bride has died, then look for an old friend of the family or another relation. It is a great privilege to be asked to carry out this important role, so think carefully about whom you ask.

Gloria: 'My dad passed away only two months before my wedding. My grandfather asked if he could take his place, and I was so pleased to agree. On the day, though, there wasn't a dry eye in the church as we walked down the aisle.'

Wanda, a young widow, told me that her own father had died when she was a child, and with trepidation she asked her father-in-law to 'do the honours' at her second wedding. She watched with horror as his eyes filled with tears, but they were tears of happiness on her behalf that she had found joy and love again.

I am afraid in this sort of situation you are likely to be subjected to pressure from all directions about doing the 'right' thing, and the worry is that the 'right' thing can depend upon where you are standing. A father might fly from the other side of the world to be at his daughter's wedding, but if it was her stepdad who was there for her over the years the poor girl becomes fraught with divided loyalties.

If only we'd known ...

'It was Victor who sat up with me when I was a kid and ill in the night, not my father – yet he is furious that I want Victor to be at my side next month.'

Connie: 'Here I am, a professional woman of forty-three. I have been married before, and yet I am in tears because my mother says that her partner should give me away, not my dad who left the family fifteen years ago.'

I say to Connie and all the other brides facing this particular dilemma: listen to what everyone has to say, consider their points of view, and then take heed to what you feel in your heart is right. In your heart you will know who you want by your side on your wedding day, so go with that. Be true to your own feelings. Speak up in good time and, if you must, say something like, 'Sorry, Dad, but I want Barry to walk me down the aisle' or 'Sorry, Barry, but I feel I want to ask Dad to do this job on my wedding day', and if they love you as much as you believe they do, they will hide their disappointment and give you their blessing. After all, you are the bride!

Divorced parents at the wedding

If your parents are divorced, there are certain things which need *very* careful handling in connection with your wedding, however old you are. As a 'child of divorce' you will already be all too aware of the delicate balance which you have probably adopted over time. Although it is said that parents divorce each other and not the children, you will know that it is by no means as simple as that. If the break-up of your parents has meant the loss of either a mother or a father, there will be grief for you that once again both your parents will not be there together for your very important day

For Elizabeth, her problems began as soon as she got

engaged. The simple task of putting a notice in the paper to announce her engagement caused so much upset that she didn't know where to turn. 'My dad didn't want his name associated with my mum's, and he said he would put in a separate notice with his partner's name. He was also furious that my intended had been married before.' Elizabeth told me that her forthcoming marriage had stirred up old grievances between her parents and she felt that as her engagement was causing so much grief she could not even begin to think of wedding plans.

If any of the parents are still in conflict over their own broken marriages it is most taxing for the couple who are marrying. As we heard from Elizabeth, this can very quickly spill over on to their own plans. Plenty of thought must be given every step of the way, and allowances made for potentially fraught situations.

Of course, there are parents who can put their own differences aside, even if only temporarily, and come together to be the parents of the bride or groom on the day of their child's wedding. You may be one of the lucky ones who know that even though your parents are not a couple, they will come together in this way. This is all that you are asking of them. And you have every right to expect divorced parents, who must have been through similar experiences themselves, to be exceptionally sympathetic at your second wedding.

Not all divorced parents can manage this, so you may have to consider a worst case scenario. As if you don't have enough to worry about and to organise, you must give time to consider how your mother and father will react when they encounter each other for the first time after many years.

Don't leave it until the last moment to decide where people sit or stand at the ceremony, or just hope that things will 'sort themselves out'. Sadly, this is not likely to happen without considerable foresight and planning on your part.

Once a divorce has split a family apart the fallout continues, often through the generations, which can have an impact on a wedding later on. As Kate told me: 'My parents divorced. Mum broke off all relations with Dad's family, and now, twenty years on, she is saying I can't have my gran (Dad's mum) at my wedding. What shall I do?'

What made this even more complicated was that Kate's fiancé, Jacob, had been married before and wanted to be married quietly in a civil ceremony. They both had agreed to ask very few guests so there was no question of being able to keep her gran apart from her mother. The pressure on Kate from her mother continued right up until the wedding day. Kate felt that there was no way she would upset her beloved gran, and only at the eleventh hour when Kate's mother accepted this, did she agree to be present at her daughter's wedding.

Kate had the courage to make the point firmly to her mother that she must *behave*. In the event all went well. Kate said they had other problems with Jacob's ex, his children, and his ex-in-laws, but it was nothing compared to the fuss that her mother made over an issue which should have been resolved many years ago.

If only we'd known ...

*'Tell brides of divorced parents to watch out,' said
Hilary. 'At my first wedding my father arrived with
his new partner, although we had all agreed
beforehand that she would not come. My mother then
refused to come on to the reception. You can imagine
the tears! And to add to that, my then husband's
mother had a stand-up fight with her ex mother-in-
law, so more tears. This time I am having none
of them at the service or reception. Learn
from my experience.'*

If your parents are divorced, one or both parents may have a
new partner with them. If at all possible, talk to each parent
well in advance and try to understand how much they do or
do not want to be in contact. Begin with the parent you feel
closest too. Once you know how they are feeling you can
plan accordingly. Hopefully, once again, you will find that
even couples who have been at daggers drawn for years will
lay aside their animosity and give their child the day of his or
her dreams.

Of course if *both* you and your partner have parents who
are divorced and have new partners, the complications
multiply out of all proportion; strategic planning then
becomes a necessity.

For Adrian and Carole it was as if they had been told to

'multiply the number you first thought of'. Adrian's father had been married three times, and all his wives wanted to see their 'beloved Adrian' married. Carole's parents had both been married twice, and her dad was now living with yet another lady. 'What shall we do?' they both cried.

The situation was complicated by the fact that some of the wives/husbands were speaking to each other and some were not. It was clear that Adrian and Carole did not have a chance of pleasing everybody, so I suggested they should decide what *they* wanted. When they had thought this through Carole decided that as her father 'gave her away' at her first wedding ten years before, this time she would walk down the aisle accompanied by her two daughters. Adrian did in fact want all his stepmothers to be invited, and so they were seated carefully in the church in different pews, and at tables far away from each other at the reception. I urged them to make sure, before the day, to keep everyone informed about who would be there, so that there would be no sudden surprises for anybody.

They decided to restrict the photographs to the bridal party. Adrian told me: 'No way are we having a squabble about who stands next to whom in the photos. No fist fights about who is mother of the groom, thank you.' As they were paying for the wedding reception themselves, they felt (and I agree) that it was quite in order not to have a line-up, but just for them to greet their guests alone. In other words, to keep things as simple as possible, with the focus on the bridal couple. Indeed, with second weddings this is usually a sensitive way to cope with 'family photographs' rather than for anyone to be embarrassed about who stands where. (An exception can be made when children are involved. See 'Children at the wedding', page 174.)

I received a frantic email from Fiona: 'My daughter is getting remarried in August. My husband and I are getting divorced because he left me for another woman. My in-laws have accepted her. I do not want to sit with either my (by then) ex-husband or his family. Where *should* I sit?'

I urged Fiona to talk to her daughter and tell her that she did not want to sit with them. It is quite understandable, and what is usual in these circumstances is for the ex and his new partner to sit further back in the church, whereas the bride's mother should sit in the front pew. She should try to have a friend or relation (of either sex) to be by her side as her escort.

Bonnie: 'Help! My parents are definitely not speaking. Wild horses won't make them even acknowledge each other. Any pointers for our wedding? They will both be there with their own "supporters".' My advice was that Bonnie's parents should be seated well apart from each other. And she should take a tip from Adrian and keep formal photographs to a minimum.

If you have divorced parents be careful that guests do not feel they are between two camps. Make sure you and your groom greet all the guests. There is no need to have either parents by your side, either at a line-up or at your table. The top table – which is often the heart of the wedding reception – can be made up of bride and groom and best man and attendants. Again, if the wedding is large enough, divorced parents can be seated at tables strategically placed at a safe distance, each surrounded by a group of people who are 'on their side'.

Christine made sure before her wedding to André that all the parents met up for a meal well in advance of the day itself: 'Even that took some organising. Both our parents are divorced and remarried. It was the first time they had all met up, and there was some initial frostiness but they thawed out and all put their minds to making our wedding day a happy one. We both had thought there might be trouble with our ex-partners, and there was, but nothing compared to what could have exploded with our parents. In fact, there was a lot to drink, and we had a jolly good party.' Christine counted herself as lucky. But, was it luck? Wasn't it more likely the result of foresight and because she grasped the nettle well in advance so that any blips could be ironed out?

Once you have decided on the plan for your wedding, it is hard for a bride or groom to say, in effect, 'Well, so be it!' But if one divorced parent or the other decides to miss the ceremony or the reception, then that is their choice. Just say to them that although you can understand their position, and you will be sad if they are unable to attend, you have to stick to the plan that both of you have decided on for your wedding day. It is not a day for old grievances in the family to be aired, but a joyous moment for you both to look towards the future.

What to wear

This question haunts many brides-to-be and is a source of uncertainty for many women marrying for the second time. 'What *is* allowed?' is the question I get asked again and again, in varying forms. Second-time brides, with experience

156

behind them, are often more confident about what suits them. One bride I spoke to had known from the age of ten exactly what she wanted to wear. Penny's first wedding had been a very quiet one, and she had just worn a trouser suit. Now, with her second wedding, she wanted the world to see her dressed as a bride. She rummaged through several trunks of discarded odds and ends to find a drawing of a dress she had designed twenty years previously at school, on a hot summer's day, with her best friend. With a cry of triumph she took it off to a dressmaker to have the gown of her dreams made into a reality.

On the other hand, whether or not to wear white for a second wedding is a powder keg often waiting to explode for a bride. Everyone has a firm opinion on this, often loudly expressed. Most people think 'not really'. However, listen to this from Tracy: 'My husband said he wanted to see me in white. At forty-four-years-old, with four grown children I didn't think it would be too appropriate.'

Again, the worry of 'What will others think?' raised its head for this bride: 'My husband said that if I wore some other colour it would seem to him as though I wasn't done with the past. He said he would feel that while I was saying my vows to him there was a part of me that was giving importance to my previous marriage. He said that by wearing white I would signify to the world that I was coming to him with a pure heart and fresh dreams.' How could Tracy possibly say 'no' after hearing that? She did wear a white dress and decided that she would not allow her past marriage to control her, or the colour of her dress.

If only we'd known ...

'Why are people so horrible? I am planning to marry again. Faces fall when I tell an assistant I am shopping for my second wedding dress. Comments such as "It will do for a second *wedding" come even from my family.'*

What to wear will depend somewhat on where you are getting married. If you are having a wedding or reception outdoors, then it is wise to reflect this in your choice of dress (and shoes!). In any case, when deciding what to wear, it is a good idea to consider what the weather is likely to be on your wedding day. A dress chosen in the summer without thought to the seasons, may be too flimsy for a winter wedding, and vice-versa.

Brides often love to wear a dress their mother or grandmother wore, and if this is what she genuinely wants, it is a lovely tradition. But I did feel concern when faced by an e-mail from Belinda about her wedding dress: 'I paid a fortune for the dress for my first wedding, and I wore it again for my subsequent marriage. I am now getting married for the third time. Can I wear it again?'

Although I firmly believe that all brides should be 'given into' with most of their desires, I felt this was a time to draw the line. Of course, in the end it was up to Belinda to decide, but she did ask me, after all! I suggested that both she and her groom might feel it was more of a fresh start to wear something else, even though she had paid a 'fortune'. If funds were tight, perhaps she could have the dress significantly altered instead to give it a new life. After all, I was sure she would not want her wedding photographs to have an air of déjà vu.

If only we'd known ...

'Don't wear gloves. They looked great when I tried on my wedding outfit, but there was confusion when I had to put on a ring, and disaster when I had to eat at the reception.'

Take heed of a tip I learned from Patti: 'I had a dream dress in my mind, but however hard I tried I couldn't get it across to my dressmaker. How I wish I had done what my sister did. She remembered my tears and frustration about my dress not turning out right, and when her time came she went out and tried on lots of gowns, found one that really suited her, and then had it copied.'

Another tip is for a bride to walk about in her dress before the wedding. One woman told me: 'I only ever stood still in front of the mirror for my fittings. On the day I found it so hard to walk with the full skirt and train, I look as if I am drunk on the video. Warn people! For this wedding I shall wear a dress I can manage and shoes I can walk in.'

The older, more sophisticated bride will also have fun selecting a gown. 'Less like a meringue, and this time a sleek silk dress with spaghetti straps for me,' said Lily. The field is wide open. You will almost certainly have a better idea of lines and colours which suit you than you did several years earlier.

Sally agreed: 'I think that for my first wedding I went over the top. This time I am wearing a cream dress with a long cream jacket over it, with matching hat and shoes. I will look like a bride – but not a first-time one!'

Paula decided that for her second wedding a garment that in some way she could wear again, rather than a wedding dress to pass on to a daughter, was what she wanted. So she chose a soft colour and went for a pale green dress. She put a shimmery lace jacket over the dress and is delighted to have two items of dressy clothes to wear again. Paula laughed when she recalled the money she spent on the dress for her first wedding – it had gone into the attic in a bag the moment the wedding was over.

Don't let your shopping expedition be spoilt by a silly misunderstanding as Juliet's was: 'Tell the assistant straight away what you are looking for and why. I just mentioned a wedding, and although I am only thirty-eight, she started talking to me as "the mother of the bride". I had to say loudly two or three times, "I am the bride – I am the bride."'

Another second-time bride, also of fairly mature years, said that when she was shopping for a wedding outfit the assistant tried to guide her towards very dowdy outfits, and when she protested was told that, 'Encore brides usually dress soberly, madam.' Another bride in tears!

If your groom has been married before, try to get a peep at the photographs of his previous wedding, so that you don't get too close to what his first bride wore. Anthea talked to me about the worries she had. She was planning her wedding to a man who had been married twice before. Anthea had seen the photographs of both his earlier weddings and felt that with one bride in flowing hippy clothes and bare feet, and the second in a traditional long-veil-and-train outfit, there was nowhere for her to go! 'Help!' read her e-mail, 'What on earth can I wear to be different?'

I suspect there may have been more to Anthea's worries than selecting an outfit. Perhaps she felt that with two ex-wives in the background comparisons would be made about everything. So, the single most important thing for Anthea to keep in mind is that she should be *herself* at all times, and this goes for deciding what to wear at her wedding. Above all, her choice must reflect the woman she is, and by giving so much attention to what the previous wives had done she was in danger of losing sight of her individuality and uniqueness. If for this reason she starts to get in a state over her wedding dress, then her anxieties will spiral upwards if she begins to worry about how her predecessors managed with cooking or sex!

There is no need to spend the earth on a dress or outfit. 'Relax,' said Selina. 'We are having a wedding on the cheap. I am wearing a green linen dress, and my daughter, who is maid of honour, is wearing a green sun-dress. My fiancé and his son will wear green polo shirts and khakis.'

Although you will want to wear something spectacular, money alone does not guarantee this. There are other ways to achieve a special effect. Search through the small ads in local papers – there are often bridal gowns and bridesmaids' dresses for sale at a fraction of their original price.

Jackie told me that she and her close friend spent many happy Saturday afternoons hunting around charity shops where they found a never-ending choice of dresses and hats suitable for a bride (and her friend). 'No one would ever have believed that the pair of us dressed for a total of thirty-five pounds, including the hats.'

There can be a lot of excitement about selecting what you will wear for your second wedding, so make sure you enjoy it. Abigail told me that for her first wedding her mother and mother-in-law thought of everything. 'My mum-in-law even borrowed a headdress for me, and my mother went and selected my bouquet. Whatever was I thinking of? But, I was very young and didn't like to say "no". This time I am off to find the outfit of my dreams. Blow the cost!'

162

A word if you are pregnant: there are very pretty dresses to wear designed in a floating, flattering way. Take time to seek them out and avoid any dress which accentuates the waist. Gone are the days when a bride with a bump had to carry a large bouquet.

One worried future mother-in-law wrote to me to ask for help with her future daughter-in-law's outfit. 'It is Lara's second wedding, and she is expecting her second child in a couple of months. I am paying for her dress. What should she wear? What is appropriate? I am very uncomfortable with her idea of a frilly gown with a long train. I see something knee-length, very plain and simple, with no train. What is the etiquette? I want to be open to her wishes.'

I had to agree with this mother-in-law that it is not usual for a second-time bride to have either a train or a veil. There are so many very pretty dresses around, and they don't have to be 'plain'. The dress can be any length she wants. She could really go to town with a very pretty hat. I hoped that they could agree, as I felt the woman who sent me the e-mail was really trying to help, but I did not hear from the prospective bride!

The only veto for second-time brides does seem to be about wearing a full veil and a long train. The consensus of opinion is that a veil, especially a long one, should be left for the first-time bride. These seem to be the only restrictions when it comes to what to wear at your wedding. So go to town, and look your loveliest.

The groom, on the other hand, whose only choice is

between formal wedding gear or just a smart suit is lucky … he can even wear something very much more informal these days, like Selina's groom's khakis!

If only we'd known …

'I wish I had worn white again. I gave in and bought a blue dress. I didn't feel like a bride at all. And I was really offended when the photographer referred to me as "the lady in the blue dress".'

'Am I allowed bridesmaids?'

Oh dear, second-time brides do worry about this: 'Can I ask the same friend to be a bridesmaid this second time?', 'I want my sister to be my bridesmaid, but she is married. Is it OK?', 'Will people think it strange if my daughters are my bridesmaids? I am a widow, but it is a first wedding for my husband-to-be', 'My future mother-in-law says it is out of the question for me to have a bridesmaid or page boy because I did the first time I was married. Is she right?' These different e-mails all reflect one of the most vexing questions for brides.

Why should this mother-in-law set herself up to know what is 'done' or 'not done'? Once more it is the same problem: this mother-in-law probably has a stronger sense of foreboding about a second marriage niggling away in the background than the question of bridesmaids. But as this is how it has come out, now is a good time to get everything into the open. Is it the whole plan for the wedding which is causing concern? Or the fact that her son is marrying a woman who has been married before? Don't let this uncertainty fester away. The chances are that if this bride 'gives way' on the bridesmaids issue, something else will crop up. In a situation like this try to find out what it is really all about.

A bride may invite anyone she wishes to be a bridesmaid, or matron of honour. If a close friend has played this role before, and she is willing, I cannot see any reason why she should not do so again. For a married sister it might be more appropriate to call her 'matron of honour', although the duties of supporting the bride will be the same. She may prefer to be dressed in a less 'bridesmaidsy' dress. In any event if you are having other, younger, bridesmaids, a matron of honour should wear something different but complementary. I recently attended a wedding where the bridesmaids, of varying ages and sizes, were all dressed in the same colour, but with age-appropriate styles and lengths.

'Do the bridesmaids walk in front of, or behind, the bride at a second wedding? I do want to get this right,' enquired Rachel.

I don't believe the position of the bridesmaids has anything to do with how many times you have been married. In America, more bridesmaids do walk up the aisle in front of the bride. Others choose to let a small girl walk in front of the bride – perhaps as a flower-girl – with older bridesmaids behind the bride and her escort.

If only we'd known ...

*'I arranged my first wedding like a military
operation. For my second I was more laid-back.
Disaster! My bridesmaids, who I took on trust,
arrived with different coloured lipstick and nail
polish which clashed with their mauve dresses. I
trusted them to coordinate. Stupid me.'*

Do be kind to older bridesmaids when selecting the colour
and style of their dresses. I am sure you know what I mean.
Also, learn from this bride: 'I took my four bridesmaids in
plenty of time to get our shoes for the wedding, and then
sent them all away to be dyed to match the dresses. On the
day of the wedding we discovered that the shoes had
shrunk, so we all hobbled down the aisle in shoes which
were too small. It is clear on the video that we are all having
trouble walking.' She went on to say that now it makes
them all laugh, but it didn't on the day!

I was told of another near calamity: 'I had coloured, one-
size-fits-all tights for my bridesmaids. As we dressed, we
found that they must have been made for children!
Pandemonium. We were nowhere near any shops, so I
decided that as it was a summer wedding we would all go
without. Great success. Thank goodness I was more relaxed
at my second wedding. Remembering my first, I think if this
problem with tights had happened then my mother and I
would both have had heart attacks.'

If you have very young children as pages or flower girls try to rehearse with them what they will have to do. Even so, be prepared for all manner of things to happen in an unexpected way on the day.

Listen, and perhaps laugh, at Juliette's experience: 'We rehearsed and rehearsed our little flower girl to scatter petals in front of me. She couldn't seem to catch on at all, so in the end I super-glued the flowers to her basket. On the day, though, she suddenly remembered what we had been trying to teach her. The only snag was the flowers were unmoveable! She wrestled with them and then put the basket upside down on her head and walked down the aisle. Everyone was in fits of laughter – even me!'

Not all brides might have been so forgiving. Numerous couples I have spoken to have said that there was an air of relaxation and ease at their second wedding which had been absent from their first.

If only we'd known ...

*'Beware of small bridesmaids with muffs. Mine put
sweets, tissues and goodness knows what in theirs, which
of course spilled out all over the aisle at the crucial
moment. I nearly died with embarrassment. Kids!'*

Try to let any children involved visit the actual venue beforehand. It can be very difficult for young kids when they are faced by a crowd of people staring at them in a setting they do not know. Also, if they are of very tender years, do make sure the clothes you decide on are going to be easy for them to wear. However cooperative a child may be at the start, you may have a problem on the day if you try to force a reluctant five-year-old boy into a page's outfit with tights. A hat which may look charming in the photographs may be too uncomfortable for a child to wear for any length of time. One of my own daughters went into a spin, aged four, when on the day we tried to curl her hair in the way the bride had decreed. So remember to keep things simple. I think putting rosebuds in the hair of small bridesmaids is a lovely idea; it's an arrangement they can then forget about, unlike an uncomfortable headdress.

Young children can be scene stealers. Some have even been known to sit down on strike when overcome by the occasion. One five-year-old, leaning forward and blowing out the unity candle, made quite a statement! So think as carefully as possible about the age and temperament of the attendants you choose. And do, *do* think carefully about who you ask. Nothing can divide a family more quickly than more children from one side of the family than the other being chosen to play a part on the day.

Consider too what will happen to any very young attendants at the reception. Will there be room for them to run around? Will there be other children to play with? What if it is a late wedding and the children get tired? There is a company which makes party bags for weddings (www.partypop-its.co.uk/weddings.htm); these are excellent and will keep young fingers occupied at strategic moments.

Another idea is to arrange for someone, either paid or not – possibly an au pair or mother's help – to entertain the children in a separate room, especially at speech time. Make enquiries when you plan your reception to see if there is another room in which small guests can let off steam.

Your *own* children as bridesmaids? There is a lot to be said about this. See 'Children at the wedding' page 174.)

Points to remember about bridesmaids at a second wedding:

- It is quite in order to have bridesmaids.
- You may care to have a matron of honour instead.
- Be kind to older bridesmaids when selecting a colour and style.
- Make sure that bridesmaids try on their complete outfit several days in advance of the wedding. Leave nothing to chance.
- If you decide on a very young child, be prepared for anything to happen!
- Give careful thought to what younger bridesmaids or pages are to wear, and keep their outfits comfortable and simple.
- Try to find a way of keeping children happy during the reception.

Children and remarriage

'Family quarrels are bitter things. They don't go according to any rules.'

F.SCOTT FITZGERALD, *Notebooks*

Do you want to be a step-parent?

You must consider this question very seriously if you are thinking of getting married to someone who is already a parent. It can be a daunting experience to take on a child from a new partner's earlier relationship. You may feel you love children to bits, but are you able to see yourself as a step-parent? And what is really involved in becoming a stepfather or stepmother?

First, it is not always easy for everyone involved to dismiss the stereotype preconceptions of the 'wicked' fairy-tale step-parents. As a result, some step-parents-to-be fall into a trap: they subconsciously blank out that this is what they may very well become in the children's minds after the wedding. I regularly hear: 'Oh, surely not. His kids don't live with him. They will only visit us', or 'I'm too young to be a stepmother', or even, 'We will be more like sisters, or friends.' Big mistake. It is unlikely that the children will be in the market for another sibling, or a new 'friend' who is not of their choosing.

If only we'd known ...

'Oh, if only we had known that a bolshy stepchild can come between a couple in six months flat. Any advice for a third marriage!!!?'

Nobody, nobody finds 'instant parenthood' easy, and preparation for a major change in status of this order takes a lot of time, willingness and patience.

> Remember that a parent and step-parent are not interchangeable, and it is unreal and unfair to expect a new step-parent to love the children (and to be loved back) unconditionally from the start. It is no good banking on 'I'm good with kids' because the children will have agendas of their own.

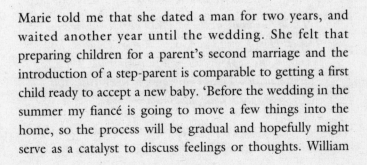

Marie told me that she dated a man for two years, and waited another year until the wedding. She felt that preparing children for a parent's second marriage and the introduction of a step-parent is comparable to getting a first child ready to accept a new baby. 'Before the wedding in the summer my fiancé is going to move a few things into the home, so the process will be gradual and hopefully might serve as a catalyst to discuss feelings or thoughts. William will also come to dinner more frequently as we draw closer to the date. It's hard work, and if you have any more suggestions, I am open to other ideas.' Marie's thoughtful preparation will surely pay off; she says she hopes to keep the family routine very stable during this time, including visiting the children's dad.

I am asked repeatedly 'What are the rules?' Step-parents all urge 'caution', 'to wait and see how the land lies' and, above all, to leave any discipline to the natural parent until you feel on really firm and solid ground. Be on the lookout for the green-eyed monster of jealousy. The kids may find it hard to share their mother or father with you and, if you are honest, you may find it hard to share your new love with them – someone in whose heart they already occupy a treasured place.

The best way forward is to wait until you accept in your innermost being that by agreeing to marry the man or woman you love, you are prepared to take on children you are in the process of getting to know and hopefully also growing to love.

If only we'd known …

'I said "no kids" at the wedding very firmly to my fiancé. How I wish I had given it more thought. Five years on, my stepkids still hold it against me. I can't think now how I could have been so insensitive and stupid. Please, please warn others.'

Very early on establish how much involvement there is likely to be with the children. Will they live with you full-time? Visit on weekends? Every weekend? Will they holiday with you? Will your new spouse have to travel miles to visit them? How often? If so, will you go too? Are you going to turn into a stepgrandparent overnight?

The daunting fact to keep in mind is that the greatest number of second marriages which do not make it are those where there are children from a previous relationship. The e-mails I receive bear witness to this. As a new husband or wife wrestles with an impossible ex over arrangements with the children, the 'new' parent may feel very much at sea: 'His ex has so much destructive power, and he is broken down by all this fighting over the children', 'Her ex-husband never gives us a moment's peace. Because of this, the children can't settle, and Gillian and I are already at each other's throats.'

There are likely to be stormy times ahead if you are about to become a step-parent. However, in the life of any family there are sure to be highs and lows, so keep this in mind when the wind blows cold. If you and your new partner discuss all issues *before* they become a problem, then there is no reason why in time you should not all be able to be a happy family.

Nothing is sadder than to see a new family torn apart by the strife and hostilities connected with a previous relationship. But it happens all too often. A parent may feel ripped in two pieces by trying to cope with the demands of both an ex wife or ex-husband and the children from their relationship. Meanwhile, the new 'step' is bewildered by just how far to make a stand. Step-parents do have rights too, so consideration should be given to the new husband or wife who is settling into the family.

Children at the wedding

When faced with becoming a step-parent, the first and most immediate problem is whether to have the children at the wedding. This is where a second wedding poses another problem which does not affect first weddings. At first weddings, the only question involving children is usually: 'Are we going to invite *any* children to the wedding and reception?' There are families who will not consider having a celebration without the children present, and yet others who go for a more sophisticated wedding and make it clear, one way or another, that children are not welcome. Sometimes the formality of the celebration, the restriction on the numbers involved, or perhaps the late hour of the wedding and reception help in making this decision. But, this is not so for a second wedding where the bride or groom already has a child or children. Then the most contentious issue is always over what should be done with the children on the wedding day.

If only we'd known ...

*'We had too many small children at the service. I wish we
had done as my brother did later, have someone who took
the children into a side room and looked after them.'*

As we have seen, a second wedding in these circumstances is
also about the creation of a new family, a stepfamily. Your
wedding will not be as it would have been if you were both
marrying for the first time, so don't pretend, even to
yourselves, that it can be. As soon as the very word 'step' has
to be used, temperatures begin to rise. Don't let the situation
develop out of hand, so make sure you have a discussion
about the children and their involvement on the actual day
very early on. The best that can be hoped for is that there will
be a natural progression from telling the children the news
about your marriage to the part they will play at the wedding
itself. It is wonderful if the children are so full of excitement
that straight away they begin to plan what they will do and
wear. And in many families this is fortunately what happens.
But what if the one who is not a parent has other ideas?

Mildred: 'Help! Quickly! We are marrying in three months'
time, and last night my fiancé just casually asked me what
part his two kids would be playing on our wedding day. I
freaked. I want a true "fairy-tale" wedding and I do not
want two kids messing it up. What can I do?'

This sort of e-mail, and many like it, comes my way with surprising regularity.

Don't let's beat about the bush: anyone marrying someone who is already a parent must face up to the fact that the commitment will be not only to a loved one but to a child or children too. Even if your partner and the children do not live together, you will find that the children cannot be excluded from your life.

Mildred was incensed by my reply, and said that as far as she could see her wedding day had nothing at all to do with Alan's children. We had quite a heated exchange of e-mails, and even when she told me that over this 'Alan was not on her side either', nothing would budge her from her stand.

Lauren wrote to say that both she and her future husband had been married before and both had children. They had discussed the idea of not having any children at the wedding, and the reason for this was that Lauren cannot 'stand' being with Tom's eight-year-old daughter. We e-mailed back and forth about this, and Lauren agreed that in her heart she knew that her children should be part of the day, however, she just did not want Tom's youngest there. 'I know,' she said, 'that she will spoil my day.'

My concern – which I shared with her – was that in later years Lauren may come to resent the little girl even more because her behaviour had prevented the inclusion of Lauren's own children at the wedding ceremony. This did the trick, because Lauren could see that this would be so. In the end, she begged a future sister-in-law to take charge of the child, by hook or by crook, on the day. I have yet to hear how Lauren and Tom's wedding day turned out.

A distraught father wrote asking for any tips to solve a

rapidly approaching disaster. 'I have been married before and have a four-year-old and a three-year-old. My bride-to-be has agreed they can be bridesmaids, but will not allow the children's mother to come and dress them. She says that her mother, who the kids do not know, will do that.

> There is real trouble on the horizon here. Very young children at a wedding – any wedding – need a great deal of supervision and support. The mother-of-the-bride is likely to have a hundred other things on her mind, apart from dressing two very young children. My mind leapt to other difficulties too. Who will actually look after them on the day?

Any bride who chooses very young children as bridesmaids has to be prepared for all kinds of mishaps. When one of my granddaughters, aged two-and-a-half, was a bridesmaid, she refused to let go of her mother's hand at the crucial moment, and my daughter had to trail after the bride holding a teddy bear and trying to look as if she wasn't there!

If only we'd known …

'My husband insisted on his kids coming to the wedding. What they did was hang around his legs, actually holding on to him. You can see them in the photos. I was so angry.'

Children at the reception do need more than just an eye kept on them, and in this father's case these very young children naturally stuck to their dad like a limpet. Even if children are rather older, they may feel a bit lost at a wedding where they do not know many people. So be sure that someone is designated to watch out for them. Remember, on the actual day you will be much too busy to do this.

'I am at my wits' end. My daughters are to be my bridesmaids, and now, a month before the wedding, my fiancé has said he wants his daughter, who is eighteen, to be a bridesmaid too. She lives two thousand miles away. I have never met her, and I couldn't get a dress made now, even if I wanted to. What shall I do?' Very real practical difficulties stand in the way for this bride-to-be. I think every effort should be made to include this daughter somehow, as goodwill goes a long way. My suggestion is that this second-time bride should pick up the telephone and try to talk this through with her stepdaughter-to-be. There must be ways around this problem; a great deal will depend upon what the others are wearing and how old they all are.

If only we'd known ...

'My wife-to-be's daughter said she didn't want to come to our wedding. I said "suits me". Ten years on I still regret these words.'

If your child does not live with you, but it is agreed by all concerned that he or she will take part in the wedding ceremony, make sure you do not give your ex too many of the additional chores all weddings generate. There are not many former spouses who are willing to go back and forth for dress fittings, track down those special shoes, and arrange a haircut at precisely the right moment. Take responsibility for organising all these details, just as you should bear the costs involved. This is particularly important if there are complicated travel arrangements to be made.

Let me repeat this about the children and the wedding day: discussions about their involvement must take place right at the beginning. You must not assume that your partner is thinking along the same lines as you are and so it is not necessary to have a discussion! Nothing could be further from the truth. As always you should remember that you should not take anything for granted over the trickier points concerning a second wedding.

How to make it a happy day for the children

If telling the children the news about your wedding has gone down well, and they want to be involved, how can they best be included? Bridesmaids, page boys, best man (or woman), flower girls and ushers are roles which immediately come to mind, and if everyone is willing there is a lot to be said for this. Even if you are having a civil wedding, it is still a good excuse to have those extra-special outfits bought for the children, as long as they are ones they will enjoy wearing.

Adam and Olivia involved their children in all the details of planning the wedding, and arranged that on the day itself their minister would add a special vow. This was so that the children could be asked if they promised to love and honour their mother's new partner. A loud and firm 'We do' was heard by all present. In turn Adam was asked if he would love and support the children from now on. He was delighted to assert with conviction 'I do.'

Lara: 'I have searched everywhere to find out how to include my two young children (five and six) in the ceremony. They view themselves as getting married too! But I can't figure out what to say during the ceremony. It is a very modest wedding.' Why not ask whoever is marrying you if the children can stand by your side? This will go a long way to making them feel included on your family wedding day. You may well find that this is quite a usual request and you may be given some new ideas too. (See also 'Family weddings' page 195.)

Some children are very proud to give the bride away. Or, as one mother corrected me, to 'accompany' their mother on her wedding day. And remember daughters can do this just as well as sons. There are some happy families who all go to the altar together.

180

Marie had another suggestion for involving the children. She said that her children wanted to be at her wedding and so she planned that her daughters, aged twelve and eight, should invite a few friends of their own to attend the reception, where at the dinner they had their own table.

If only we'd known ...

'Watch the kids and the booze. We didn't, and had five stepchildren who had to be carried up to their beds when it was all over.

Cindy, who had two daughters of her own and was marrying Bill who had three daughters, found a way of turning the whole wedding into a hive of activity. Luckily, all the girls loved being creative and involved with making things. She asked their advice, and then they set to, to make wedding favours, headdresses and table decorations. The more the girls became involved in the planning, the more excited they became, and, more importantly, the more in touch with each other as stepsisters. Visit www.todays weddings.com for some wonderful, inventive ideas if you are clever with your hands.

When I asked for suggestions from couples who are already married, about how children – of all ages – can take part in a wedding, I was amazed at how original some of the ideas were. Some older children prefer to be heard but not seen, so are happy to sing at a parent's wedding. Others may offer to contribute by reading a poem which can be incorporated into the service. Rosemary played a harp as her mother remarried. One daughter volunteered to paint a scene showing the whole 'new' family which decorated a wall in the church hall where they held the reception.

Children love to be consulted about details, so encourage them to suggest colours, flowers and even music, even though their taste might be in question. Ten-year-old Robin said he wanted to provide bubbles. And so he did. It was arranged for him to work a bubble machine when his mother and her new husband came out of the church.

Tommy: 'We agreed on a small, very quiet wedding, but once the kids got involved, I found I was ordering a band, someone to organise games for the children, balloons and all kinds of things we hadn't bargained on. I must say, though, we had the most wonderful wedding.'

> 'We need more flowers,' said nine-year-old Emily. Her idea, which was 'approved', was that she should stand at the door and give each guest on their arrival a flower. And why not? It might not be a usual tradition, but people were charmed by this happy little girl handing out roses.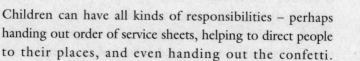

Children can have all kinds of responsibilities – perhaps handing out order of service sheets, helping to direct people to their places, and even handing out the confetti.

(Although remember to ask in good time if confetti is allowed. Alternatives which may be acceptable are wild-flower seeds, rose petals or rice.)

Of course, children are often shy, so be sure to have some 'behind the scenes' jobs available. One job could be to accompany the official photographer, because, although you may have already given a list of the photographs you want taken, it is often hard for the photographer to round up different family members. The child will be able to point out who 'Uncle Roy' is or to remember how many bridesmaids there are.

If only we'd known ...

'A year ago I e-mailed you to say you were wrong
about including children with the wedding. I am
writing now to say you were right, and months on they
will not forgive us for not letting them take part.'

If you are having a reception at home, the children can be even more inventive and, for example, will love filling clear glass vases with water coloured to match your scheme with a floating candle on top. Or help to wind tulle and ivy around the tables and door frames. Any 'hands on' ideas you can have will make them feel a part of it all. Dogs can wear fancy collars to match your colour scheme, and any reception is improved by a happy band of small but willing waiters passing round the snacks. Indeed, as Caitlin found, her children helped her choose the menu and some guests were taken aback to be offered gingerbread men, jelly, and little fancy cakes made lovingly by small hands the day before.

Points to remember about marrying someone who already has children:

- Although this is *your* wedding day, if your partner already has a child you are marrying a family.
- Make sure a photograph is taken of you all on the day. Remember you are beginning to create memories and a history for your new family.
- Listen to their suggestions. They will have ideas which will surprise you.
- Find an appropriate job for each child.
- Give each child a well-chosen gift as a 'thank-you' memento of the wedding.

How many on the honeymoon?

This question may make you blink. But, with children in the picture, planning a honeymoon may not be as simple as you think. Get all the help you can. Other members of the family can be very useful on these occasions. You may remember we heard from Abigail (page 125) that her sister took the kids to another hotel after the wedding reception to give the couple some privacy. Grandparents, too, can be very helpful on these occasions!

If you or your partner's children are involved in the wedding plans, you might be shocked, as Kevin was, when his son asked, 'Where are we going for our honeymoon?' Kevin thought that perhaps they had gone too far in talking about *our* wedding and he asked me what he should do. It was obviously time for a re-think; he needed to look at what options were on hand. Eventually it was decided that Kevin and his bride would leave the reception for a long weekend in a hotel, and then be joined by their children for a week on the coast. It was a good solution: the couple got their romantic long weekend, and as a family they all celebrated with a seaside holiday.

'No, no, no,' said Belinda. 'His ex-wife says that if the kids come to the wedding they have to stay with us for the whole week. Oh, it's so unfair.' Belinda had never expected to have to face a situation like this, but marrying a man with kids means that it is just the kind of problem that does arise.

'With six kids between us,' Jo told me, 'we knew there was no chance of a honeymoon.' But during the reception at their home they were surprised by family and friends who had booked them into a local hotel for the night. On their return, they found exhausted babysitters who had also done most of the clearing up! Good friends, indeed.

Blending families

Pillow talk may mean that you have convinced each other that *two* sets of children will be no more complicated than one. But, you will probably already have experienced different reactions from the children which indicate that it is not all going to be plain sailing. You may have been thrown into quite a spin as children of different ages react in different ways. Hopefully, some will be ecstatic at the thought of another brother or sister, but more likely others will be less than delighted at the thought of having to share everything, including one of their parents, with other children; to find you are no longer an 'only' or the baby of the family produces mixed emotions.

Let's just hope that all has gone well so far, and you have managed to negotiate through the wedding day by including all the children one way or another, with no one child seen as the star. You have cleared through this particular minefield and the marriage is behind you, and now the whole task of settling down and blending the family will begin. I can't hope to cover all that this entails in this book, but the next two sections will, I hope, provide you with some guidelines for starting off in the right direction.

Who lives where?

I am sure you will have given a great deal of thought to where your children from previous relationships will be living. Few second-time couples are fortunate enough to be able to afford a new home, so decisions will have to be made about where you will live. Like Marie, you may have decided that your second husband will move into your home after the wedding so as not to disrupt the lives of your young children who live with you.

If all the children are to be under one roof, there will be quite a bit of shifting around. Don't make assumptions, and listen to what the children themselves have to say. They may come up with something quite inventive. As I heard from Val: 'How do you cram two adults, four kids, two dogs and two cats into a very small house?' She answered her own question: 'With difficulty. Until my eldest son came up with the idea of building partitions in the biggest bedrooms, which gave all the kids their own space. Never mind that David and I had to "pig" it in the smallest room. But it worked in a way we would never have thought of.'

If only we'd known ...

'Easy now with hindsight, but how we wish we had not moved my youngest daughter into Bob's eldest's room when he was away at college. It caused the most awful ructions.'

If, on the other hand, some of the children live with you both full-time, while others come to visit, the stresses and strains will be different. It is always upsetting if you are trying to get a family settled and some or all of the children disappear from time to time to stay with the 'other' parent. Indeed, heads can spin with the organisation which is necessary when some kids are going off for the weekend and others are coming to stay. Especially so at holiday times. So planning ahead is vitally important, and hopefully the 'other' parent will cooperate.

It might be that you have not taken on board the extent that the 'other' parent will feature in your lives: Elsie said that she found it hard to believe, even one year on from their wedding, just how awkward her husband's former wife could be over childcare arrangements. 'The plans change, and change back again. Fred is so frightened of losing contact with the kids, he just says "OK" to whatever she proposes. It drives me mad.'

Lizzie: 'Because my husband's first wife is discourteous and rude, my stepchildren think they can be too. It has got worse not better since the wedding.'

If you become a step-parent, take care not to be too full of moans about the kids and your new partner's ex. Try to weather these times *together* and to prevent them becoming an issue between the two of you. I get enough e-mails from 'steps' at the end of their tether to be well aware that this is a very dangerous moment for any second marriage. 'I feel like a spare wheel' is a typical resentful statement, and 'Does a new wife/husband have any rights at all?' Yes, of course they do. But coping with children who do not want to be cooperative can be hell, and a second wife or husband will need to be very careful that the marriage is not sabotaged over this. While the natural parent can feel torn in different directions, keep in mind that the new spouse will be in an even more difficult position, constantly feeling vulnerable and uncertain about his or her role.

It is said that a stepfamily takes ten years to settle. But take heart, there are very many happy families who have managed to bond together. All the parents who spoke to me said that it didn't just 'happen'. Working together, talking endlessly, and sharing whatever came their way, were the keys to success. At your darkest hour you should remember that it isn't always easy to be a stepchild either.

How to be a stepchild

Just spare a moment for the child who is told that a parent is to remarry. There are plenty of advice sites on the Internet for second wives (http://secondwivescafe.com), and for step-parents (http://sfhelp.org), but very little help immediately available for their children.

Some kids let you know right away whether they think a wedding is a good idea or not. But others have difficulty in expressing their emotions and clam up; it is only too easy to take their silence as approval. You may believe that the news of your remarriage has had no impact on your children or you may feel that it is not their business anyway, and in this way you may have convinced yourself that they are OK. But, it is more than likely that they are not.

Children who have already become accustomed to moving between parents and who have managed to keep some kind of balance, may be nervous that by showing pleasure at the news, they will hurt their other natural parent. Of course, they may be quite mistaken. But make sure any child you know is not caught in this dilemma.

At first I was surprised to hear on my website, www.familyonwards.com, from children themselves, some as young as eleven or twelve, who had logged on and read my article 'How to be a stepchild'. This title struck a chord with many of them. I had many heartbreaking e-mails from children who said they were afraid of, hated by, and certainly didn't love their step-parent. The cry was always the same, a despondent 'I don't know what to do.' I heard from kids who had just been told they had a 'new mother' or 'new dad' or that 'Ginia' or 'Ted' would be coming to live with them.

> I heard from children who were convinced that step-parents loved only their own children, and had no time for a stepchild. I heard from others who felt abandoned in no-man's-land when a new baby was on the way.

When a child is presented with a fait accompli what is he or she to do? They are likely to be too unsure to discuss their feelings, even with their closest friends. Although stepfamilies are more and more common nowadays, it does not mean that everything always goes smoothly. As we have seen, an unfamiliar man or woman on the scene may have some trouble making friends with the children of their new partner. However, it is equally hard for a child when he is introduced to someone who is going to be a permanent member of the family from now on. So even at this exciting time in your life, be on the watch for the children. You may be dazzled at the prospect of a new beginning, but children feel quite helpless and often very alarmed at the thought of big changes ahead. If it is awkward for you to talk to your child about how they feel, make sure they do have someone they can discuss these fears with. If the children are at school, be sure to tell their teachers about the change in the family circumstances.

As I have already mentioned, children of any age are affected by the remarriage of a parent. Patricia, who is herself now a mother of thirteen-year-old twins, told me how difficult she found it to get used to a stepmum. She believed her father expected the family to accept his new bride in a 'heart-beat'. At the time, Patricia was still grieving over the death of her mother, and felt everything went too fast. But what was she to do? Her father was obviously very happy, and Patricia felt she was behaving like a 'bolshy adolescent', which wasn't what she wanted to be. It took all her willpower for her to look happy at the wedding, and she shed many tears afterwards because she felt her father never once acknowledged that the new relationship she had to accept was in any way difficult for her.

Take heart, though, because we all know families where

stepchild and step-parent have formed the most wonderful, loving bond. Just don't rush it.

How to help your children become stepchildren:

- Give it time before introducing your intended as a prospective step-parent.
- Acknowledge to each other that it can't be easy to be a stepchild.
- Make certain your child does not feel he is creating a rift with his other natural parent by celebrating your wedding.
- Make sure you both have some time alone with each child.
- Ensure someone keeps an eye on how they are feeling.
- Never say anything detrimental about the 'other' parent, however sorely you are tried.
- Listen to what your stepchild is, or isn't, saying.

9

Wedding traditions

'Custom, then, is the great guide of human life.'
DAVID HUME, *An Enquiry Concerning Human
Understanding*

What's in a name?

The custom of the bride changing her surname to that of her husband after marriage is a long-standing one. But this is no longer to everyone's taste, especially today when many women are anxious about losing their identity by becoming overnight 'Mrs New-Husband'. The situation is exacerbated in second weddings where there is a first wife whose name this already is.

'I don't want to take my husband-to-be's name. There are already two other women who have done that!' Jane told me.

'I hate the idea of changing my name again. First my father's, then my first husband's and now I am expected to do it again. Do I have to?' No, Wendy, you do not have to do this.

You could follow the example of many women who have made their mark professionally when they marry for the second time. A solution often adopted is for them to be known socially as 'Mrs New-Husband' while they keep their own name in their professional field. A good example of this is that of the Prime Minister's wife, Mrs Tony Blair, who as a QC is known professionally as Cherie Booth. Other brides decide to add their name to that of their husband and so, on marrying Mr Green, Ms Brown becomes Mrs Brown-Green, with or without the hyphen.

For a woman with children who is marrying a second time, the situation is even more complex. It affects the children in a big way if they have to change their surname, so many second-time brides opt for combining the last names. It is only fair to take the children's views and those of the other parent into consideration; I recommend having a family conference, when you both can listen to what they have to say.

> Tracy: 'I wouldn't want to have a different name to my children. My new husband understood this, and it was a happy way out for us to join our names. The children liked it too. I would never ask them to change their names, they have their father's name and I keep it out of memory for him. He died when they were babies.'

There are other alternatives out there if you are looking for them: for instance, some couples agree the man will take the wife's last name, and even some who combine one or two of the syllables of each of their names to make a new one. You should also not act too precipitately, as a bride has to wait until she actually has a marriage certificate before she can use her married name.

Remember that there are many different official bodies who will have to be told about your change of name. One tip is to make a note of everyone who sends you mail for a month before the wedding and notify all of them. You may be surprised at how many people, whom you had not thought of, will need to be informed of your change of name.

Checklist of who will need to be notified of your new surname:

Bank, solicitor, electoral role, clubs of which you are a member, doctor, dentist, passport office, driving licence and car registration office, store accounts, credit cards, building societies, subscription magazines and professional organisations and journals are the main ones to contact. But don't forget friends and family who may need to be updated on your new name or address ... and even your ex and his/her family if you are still in touch with them!

Family weddings

In an earlier chapter I related how all research shows that children find it easier to feel part of the new family if they have been included in the wedding plans and ceremony, and I showed my admiration for the many couples who go to enormous lengths to make the children feel that it is 'their' day too.

I am all in favour of the rather pleasing custom, which is beginning to take off, of giving the children at their parent's second marriage a 'family medallion'. The family medallion is a piece of jewellery – a pendant, ring or lapel pin – and the symbol engraved on it is of three equally merged circles. The first two represent the marriage union and the third the importance of *children* in the family. The presentation of a medallion to each child is often incorporated into the service, thus denoting that this is a *family* wedding; and by letting the children take part in the ceremony that a new family is coming together, not just a couple.

The ceremony for a family medallion, which lasts no more than five minutes, can easily be integrated into any religious or civil wedding service. After the couple exchange rings, their children join them for this special observance focusing on the family nature of remarriage.

The idea for this medallion came from Dr Roger Coleman, a clergyman in the US, who performs marriage ceremonies specifically designed to include children when a parent remarries. Coleman says that 'the traditional wedding ceremony does not serve the needs of couples with children from a previous relationship. That's because traditional weddings focus exclusively on the union of a man and a woman. The important role of existing children and the family nature of remarriage is simply ignored.' He reminds us that 'family weddings', where at least one of the couple is already a parent, are no longer the rarity they were a few years ago. In fact, now the bride or groom has young children in as many as one in three marriages.

The medallions have been designed for couples of all faiths to use and Dr Coleman can be contacted by e-mail at rcoleman@clergyservices.com. Have a look at his website, www.familymedallion.com for more information.

Alice: 'I have just been told about family medallions. Our wedding is only a few weeks away. Are they a good idea?' I believe that anything which helps children bridge the gap from one family to another is to be welcomed. If nothing else, it makes it easier for them to talk about *our* wedding day rather than *your* wedding day.

Robert told me he had 'searched and searched' for any idea to include his child in his forthcoming wedding ceremony. 'I don't want Roland there just as an observer, I want him to feel part of it all. So does my bride.'

Bill: 'What can we do? We have planned to give medallions at our wedding. I have two kids, Ruthie has three. But my eldest son has said he doesn't want one, and won't even take part in the ceremony.' I can only assume from this message that the other children welcome the idea. Bill did not tell me how old his son is and there may be many reasons for the boy's non-cooperation. It may be that he feels he is betraying his mother in some way by accepting the medallion. Probably he does not yet feel ready to be part of a blended family, even in a symbolic way. The wise thing to do may be just to keep his medallion on one side, and hope that one day he will feel able to accept it. I don't think it would help anybody to insist that he should take part in this family ceremony.

From Alan I heard that at his wedding to Marge, who has a ten-year-old son, 'An additional vow was included and I said to Benny: "I give you this gift as a symbol of my love and as a promise to love and care for you."' At a signal from his mother, Benny walked up and stood between Alan and Marge. Alan heard afterwards that even relations who had been opposed to his remarriage to a mother with a child found the ceremony of commitment very moving.

Kenny could remember that when his mother remarried, he sat alone in a pew watching the ceremony – 'the loneliest moment of my life'. When Kenny remarried he recalled the pain of this experience and made sure that at his second wedding his daughters stood by his side as he made his vows.

It is as well to remind ourselves once again that, for many couples, a remarriage is not just joining together two people, but bringing together a family with more than one child as well.

The lighting of a Unity Candle during a wedding service is another recent addition to traditional wedding rituals. It is non-denominational and has no religious significance at all. Over the last fifteen years it has gained in popularity, and I think it is a rather pleasant addition to any ceremony since it is intended to symbolise when two become one. Or, as I have heard from many parents, when two become three, four or more! The Unity Candle is another feature where there are families joining together and where the couple getting married want to demonstrate to the children that this is a family occasion, and want to include the children in the ceremony.

There is no 'set' place in the order of service for the candle to be lit, but what is most usual is for it to be done immediately after the vows have been said. Some couples decide to invite parents and even grandparents to take part in the lighting of the candle so as to demonstrate the continuity of the family.

198

There is a wide choice of candles available, from plain white candles to very ornate ones decorated with lace and pearls.

If you want to light a Unity Candle, be sure to check in good time with the person who is marrying you. There are some rabbis and priests who do not like this innovation, but it is welcomed by others as a symbol of two people, or families, joining together. Again, the Internet provides numerous sites where you can purchase the candle.

If only we'd known ...

'Whatever you do, ask if a candle can be included in the ceremony. We left it until the very last moment and offended our clergyman, who was a really nice guy and up until then had been really helpful.'

Other customs

One new custom is to place instant cameras on the tables for guests to take photographs which later on provide amusing, and often unsuspected, reminders of the day. Another new idea – which has developed from the practice of planting a tree to mark a special occasion – is to present each guest with a 'tree in a box' – or rather a seed which will turn into a tree. As the tree grows it will, hopefully, be a reminder to your guests of a lovely day and of your growing happiness together. The boxes can be personalised with the names of the bride and groom, and are available in different colours. Contact www.branchservicesirl.bigstep.com or www.tree inabox.com for more information.

Even if they have not performed the mother-of-the-bride duties this time around, a rather lovely custom is to present a mother, mother-in-law or stepmother with some flowers; it is a token of love and appreciation.

A more traditional custom is for the bridal couple to give small gifts of little parcels of five sugar almonds, usually placed on the table, to all their guests. But do remember, each almond stands for a wish: health, wealth, longevity, happiness and ... fertility! One couple told me of the fun their guests had because of the 'conversation hearts' put on all the tables as an alternative to sugar almonds. See www.bridallinks.com if you want details about these.

Second-wedding invitations

Most second weddings are paid for by the two people getting married rather than their parents, and this is where you may feel you can be more inventive and choose something less traditional than the formal invitation sent out by the parents of a first-time bride. Of course, your parents may want to do this again, but on the whole most second-wedding invitations are sent from the couple. Almost all of the brides and grooms I spoke with said they were sending the invitations in their own names. 'After all, we are the hosts,' said Charles.

However, there were some who, although paying most of the expenses, wanted to include their parents as the hosts on the invitation. Therefore I was told of invitations which read thus:

Ann Davis and Edward Jones [the bride and groom]
together with
Mr and Mrs Cyril Smith [the bride's parents]
invite you to their wedding on ...

Anthea and Richard went one step further and decided to put the names of *both* their parents on their invitation as a mark of respect, even though, as they said 'We paid for it all ourselves.'

Although you may decide to send an unconventional invitation, one perhaps designed by yourselves, or even an invitation e-mail, do think it through first. It is important to choose the right style of invitation because it sets the tone for the kind of wedding you are planning. And avoid novel ideas which confuse or make people feel uneasy.

If only we'd known ...

'I wanted the invitations to my second wedding to be different. I enclosed a handful of confetti in each envelope. I heard much later that people hated it, but I thought at the time it would be fun.'

Your invitation must provide all the information your guests will need. Not only the date, time, place of the ceremony, but also where the reception will be. Remember that it is also imperative that you convey to your guests what kind of wedding you are planning. Friends and family will need to know if they are attending a formal or informal wedding, and nothing can make guests feel more uneasy than to arrive wearing the wrong clothes. It can be as embarrassing to be at a formal wedding wearing jeans, as it is to be at a relaxed garden wedding wearing full morning dress. So be kind to your guests. Make it clear, too, whether they will be getting a banquet or just a wine and cake reception. Be sure to include a map if either of the venues are difficult to find, and it might be as well to give some information about the availability of parking.

Have you made a decision over the vexed question of whether guests who have children are invited to bring them? Be prepared for this one in advance. As I have already mentioned, some families find it inconceivable to celebrate a wedding without children present. But by inviting the children to the reception your numbers will swell considerably and bills will mount substantially. It will also mean you have to give some thought to whether you will provide any entertainment specifically for adolescents and young children. Don't even think of putting 'no children' on the invitation; if this is what you want just be prepared to say you have decided to have an 'adult' wedding when you are asked. Any children over sixteen, whom you are inviting to the wedding, should have their own invitations.

Julian: 'We knew there would be lots of kids at our wedding, so on the invitation we added "bring your swimsuits", and they did.'

I have heard of many wedding receptions planned around a swimming pool, with guests urged to come prepared to have a splash. But do take care about safety, as on such occasions pools and small children raise a host of problems. Make sure well in advance you have someone who agrees to keep an eye on safety and take responsibility for this – and not to overdose on the champagne! Don't leave this until the last minute in case you can't find anyone who will take on this burdensome task. The best idea of all may be to hire a professional life-saver. Enquire at your local swimming pool.

Very often, people can be extraordinarily lax about replying – even to a formal invitation – and if there is no mother-of-the-bride or wedding coordinator at your shoulder, it will be left to you to telephone those who haven't had the courtesy to reply in good time. This is always embarrassing but if you have a caterer who needs to know about numbers there is no way round it. Also, with the postal service being what it is, invitations can go astray.

Caroline: 'We sent all our invitations by e-mail, fax or pager, and asked people to RSVP in the same way. And they did!'

One of the most unusual wedding invitations I was told about was from Barney. He said there had been so much argument about the wording that in the end they just sent out a simple invitation to a party. It wasn't until after the guests had arrived that they said they were getting married ... then, at that very moment! The guests were then taken into a separate room at the hotel where the ceremony was performed.

So you see, you have plenty of freedom to decide on just what you both want!

If only we'd known ...

'Take care. Once we got the bit between our teeth we telephoned everyone we knew and invited them. Of course, a few days later we realised we had forgotten just who we had invited and had no idea who was able to come or not.'

Gifts for second-time couples

A very common enquiry sent my way is: 'Should an encore bride register for gifts?' Opinions are very mixed. People are even divided about whether to give or receive gifts for a second or subsequent marriage at all!

Is it a *first* wedding for the bride and *second* for the

groom? Or vice-versa? Have they both been married before, or been living together, so that they are likely to have set up a home? Did you attend one of their first weddings and give a generous gift? All these factors play a part.

The reasons for friends and family giving handsomely to a first marriage is to help the newly-weds on their way to gather the hundred-and-one things everyone needs to make a home. With many second-time weddings it may well be that at least one or both of them already has most of the items they need. However, it should be remembered that this is not always the case, since an acrimonious divorce can leave one partner with virtually nothing in the way of household essentials. Also there are couples who really do want to make a fresh start, and prefer not to use anything from their 'old' lives. Individual circumstances play a large part in answering the question of gifts, not just for the guests but for the couple themselves.

Mary: 'Would it be appropriate to register for gifts for my second wedding? We both have little to bring together, and would love to start out fresh. I have to tell you, my mother and mother-in-law are against us doing this.'

Andrea: 'No way would I use my old china and bedding. I told guests where my bridal list was, and people on the whole were very generous. I think they understood where I was coming from. Friends who didn't just sent a kind of token gift, and that was all right too. Tell brides to do what they want to about wedding gifts.'

Alicia: 'I am getting married for the fourth time, and I don't expect gifts. Should I put this on the printed invitation?'

I think this is probably unwise. Alicia would be better advised to let the word spread through the grapevine that she does not wish to receive gifts. Adding a message of this kind to the printed invitation is rather heavy-handed, as it implies that you assume guests are going to send a gift!

If you are a friend or relative worrying about what is expected of you, are there any guidelines you should follow over this vexed question of second-wedding gifts? If you have strong feelings about divorce and remarriage, some unconscious forces may be at work to influence you, otherwise there is no particular pattern you have to follow.

Susie sent me this e-mail: 'Could you please let me know an appropriate sum of money to spend for a second wedding (bride second, groom first). The bride is a friend of the family and I did give her a significant gift first time around.' There is no set rule to follow here, but given these circumstances I suggested that Susie should be inventive and give a celebration gift which need not cost the earth. If the bridal couple have a garden, why not a shrub or small tree? If all else fails, why not a bottle of champagne or sparkling wine or an unusual house plant? I don't think there is a need for her to push the boat out again.

If only we'd known ...

*'I did not agree with the plans my brother made for
his remarriage: I sent a bread-knife. But afterwards
I felt a bit mean.'*

'We are pensioners and sent all our nieces and nephews
good wedding presents for their weddings. Now *second*
wedding invitations are arriving, and quite frankly we
haven't the cash. Should we refuse the invitations and
therefore feel we do not have to send a gift?'

I think it would be sad for this couple to miss out on
family occasions because of embarrassment over a gift.
Again, a token gift (perhaps something found in a shop 'on
sale') would be quite appropriate and, I am sure,
appreciated by the couple.

The couple should keep in mind that people require some
guidance about what they should do and what is expected of
them. So, if the bride does register a wedding list
somewhere it is evident that she is open to wedding gifts of
the more traditional kind, even if it is not necessary for you
to comply by buying something on her list. And, of course,
if there is no list, then it is up to the guest to make the
decision about what to send. And this – I am afraid – is the

advice I always give the many 'friends' who write to me complaining about having to pay for another gift, when they remember all too clearly how much they spent on either the bride or groom at their first wedding.

The sensitive bride, if registering for gifts a second time, will make sure some less expensive items are on her list. This makes it easier for friends who are a little grieved at buying another wedding gift.

It is quite in order for the bride to be open about letting her guests know that 'your presence is requested, not your presents'. Or there are other solutions, such as that of the bride who told me she invited guests to bring along a dish to share at her pot luck reception. But the most sensitive way to let people know what you are feeling is by word of mouth.

'A friend is getting married for the third time. We are not invited to the ceremony, but they are having a celebration in a smart restaurant later that week. Do I have to send a gift?' Well, no. Nobody 'has' to send a gift. But it is nice to celebrate a wedding as a guest, so flowers either sent before or after the dinner would be a very pleasing gesture.

Chloe asked for my help: 'We are marrying in London but then going to live in Canada. Can I ask people for money, as we don't want to take masses of things back with us to Montreal?' If a bride is asked whether she would like a gift or cash, it is quite in order to explain how it is difficult and expensive to transport gifts abroad and a cheque would be wonderful. But I am not really comfortable with the idea of starting out asking for money. Sensitive guests will probably discover for themselves that this is the best solution, while others will take advantage of the Internet to order wedding presents which can be delivered in Canada.

If only we'd known ...

'I wish I'd thought more about our wedding present list. After all, we already had a home together. So something to spoil us would have been better than more bloody toasters.'

Above all, no one should let the giving or receiving of presents become an issue. If you are a second-time bride or groom and you notice that gifts this time around are not so lavish as you remember for your first wedding, don't take it amiss; few people have bottomless pockets. Don't take it as a signal that friends and family are not wholeheartedly in favour of this union; economic factors are more likely to have come into the picture. If you are a friend who has only recently met with the couple and not been in any way involved with their earlier weddings, then be generous and don't hold back.

'Do what I did,' cried the somewhat mercenary Gloria.

'Marry in Japan as I did, and you will find incredibly generous Japanese family and friends all give money. It paid for our wedding.'

If you are strapped for cash, there are other solutions. A guiding principle is to choose something which will be particularly appreciated because it has been specially picked with the couple in mind, even though it didn't cost a fortune. After all, we are all more likely to remember a gift which we can see was sensitively chosen with ourselves in mind, rather than one more toaster or set of china. An alternative is to send a 'promise'. This could be a promise to help in the garden for a specific number of hours, to baby-sit (if appropriate!) or any number of things you know the couple would like to redeem at a future date. You could have a lot of fun thinking this one up.

Above all, neither bride nor groom nor any of the guests should let the giving or receiving of gifts cloud this happy time.

Speeches at second weddings

As we have seen, the second-wedding couple are not bound by many of the traditions which seem to be taken for granted for a first wedding. Deciding who will make the speeches, if indeed there are to be speeches at all, is one of them. And this can be a welcome relief, too, for many people. As the field is open, make sure you choose with care and deliberation. Make sure the person you ask to toast your health – and who will almost certainly take this to mean that he or she can tell a few jokes at the expense of bride or groom – is sensitive to the second-wedding situation. There are people who think it is amusing to start off by saying something along the lines of 'Third time lucky, Brian?' or 'Well, here we all are again …' or other clichés to remind everyone that they are celebrating *another* wedding for the bride or groom. I have heard of many similar 'jokes' being made, so ensure that this does not happen to you. Be quite open about this when you ask a friend or relative to make a speech.

Do not ask anyone to make a speech simply because you understand it is 'expected' that they have to be asked. And don't feel hidebound to choose someone of the 'right' sex! A woman friend will do equally as well as a man. Moreover, if either bride or groom have a child who would like to make a speech and who is up to it this can give a wonderful start to the new family. At one wedding I attended last year (a second for the groom), his fourteen-year-old daughter asked the guests to toast the bridal couple, and her *short*, and tactful words wishing them happiness and health in the future was a superb example of the right emphasis and sensitivity for the occasion.

If only we'd known ...

*'If only I'd known that my groom's best friend hated
me, I would not have let him speak at our wedding.
As it was, he make joke after joke about my weight,
knowing full well that I was pregnant, although it
was a big secret from the family at the time.'*

Heather: 'The worst moment of my first wedding was the
speech by the best man. He was drunk, and went on and on
and on. We couldn't stop him, and my mother was furious.
This time I have asked my brother just to ask people to raise
their glasses and drink to our future, and no more.' Another
first-class example of learning from experience.

If only we'd known ...

*'My horrible new brother-in-law referred to me in his
speech as "Clever Puss". He knew I hated that name,
and I never thought to make a point of it earlier
and to forbid it!'*

We did choose with care this time, or so we thought. On the day, however, our best man was so nervous nobody heard what he was saying, and people even began talking among themselves. We were so embarrassed,' said Ethan.

'I made our best man rehearse with me beforehand. At my first wedding the best man got my name wrong, and I burst out crying. Looking back, I think it was an omen things would go wrong,' said Naomi.

One bride refused to take a risk that anything would go wrong this time. 'I'll make the speech myself,' said Norma, and she did.

Think hard about whether you should have an interpreter if you marry in a foreign country. Ann had a professional interpreter at her wedding, but there was a huge fight with the father of the groom about it. He would not let his speech be translated, which, according to Ann, turned out to be a good thing. 'If,' she said, 'my dad had understood what he said he would have busted open my father-in-law's head right there in the middle of the banquet hall.'

Like everything else connected with the wedding, speeches need to be thought about and plans made and *agreed* upon. In fact, if you don't want speeches at all, don't have them. This is the kind of freedom which comes with a second wedding.

If only we'd known ...

*'Remember everyone has a video camera nowadays, so
any slip-up or embarrassing moment is going to be
recorded for posterity. My father-in-law got drunk,
and in the middle of a speech he gradually
disappeared under the table. This later turned up
on TV! Most people thought it was funny.
My husband didn't.'*

Second-wedding cakes

What has happened to the white, tiered traditional fruit
wedding cake with a miniature bride and groom on the top?
I can remember when the only choices before a bride were
whether to have a square cake or a round one, and to decide
upon how many tiers she wanted. There is now a much
greater variety of cakes for all weddings, not just second
ones.

Now the sky's the limit, and an exciting array of
'designer' cakes are on offer. For some brides it is an
opportunity to continue a theme running through the
whole reception, so if your idea of fun is to have a wedding
cake in the shape of a car or a dragon, you will have no
difficulty in getting one made to order.

You can select from carrot cake, chocolate cake and

sponges. I recently saw a beautiful wedding cake where the tiers were completely iced over to resemble a mountain, with sugar flowers for decoration all cunningly disguising a rich chocolate sponge inside. This very successfully blended the tradition of a white cake with the requirements of the more modern sweet tooth. There are cakes decorated with spots, stars, glitter and feathers, with fresh flowers, with silk flowers and – in the words of one cake company (which can be contacted by e-mail on: specialcake.co@cs.com) – 'an explosion of stars'.

You might even feel in the mood to emulate the chocolate wedding cake chosen by Paul McCartney – but beware, it is rumoured to have cost £1,000. Another idea for a cake with a difference is the *croque en bouche* – a French tradition of cream puffballs piled on top of each other to make a pyramid.

If only we'd known ...

'Oh! Oh! Oh! We didn't know that you have to be a really good chef to make a croque en bouche *– you know, the pyramid of creamy pastries – instead of a traditional wedding cake. I ordered it and during the reception it very slowly began to collapse, and in the end all the guests were watching this disaster-in-the-making, instead of us!'*

Have you heard of sugar sculptures? If you are looking for a 'wacky wedding sculpture', take a look at www.wacky weddingsculptures.co.uk. It seems the sky is the limit.

One couple had the novel idea of providing a tiny white iced cake for each guest. These made stunning table decorations as well as helping to create a wedding with a difference. 'After all,' said third-time bride Molly, 'how many traditional wedding cakes can you cut?' Good point, I thought.

10

Happily ever after

Ah, my beloved, fill the cup that clears
To-day of past regret and future fears.
EDWARD FITZGERALD, *Omar Khayyam*

Falling in love again

'Happy is the bride the sun shines on' is a phrase which trips off the tongue. But you will know by now that you and your partner will need more than a balmy day to make your wedding go the way it should – brimming over with affection, love and laughter.

If only we'd known ...

'I felt there was a jinx on my second wedding day. It was pouring with rain, a bridesmaid got chickenpox, the hairdresser was taken ill, and the car taking me to the service broke down. But, whereas my first wedding was flawless in every detail, this was the most wonderful day of my life.'

You will have passed through troubled waters, so there is often a feeling of relief and a cry of 'We made it!' once a second wedding day is over. You will both know that a relationship can all too easily turn sour and finish with tears. No first marriage ends without some sorrow, even if it is only grief that early dreams did not materialise. And when a loving relationship has ended in the death of a husband or wife, then you will know what it is like to go on living with a heavy heart. So, for whatever reason, there may have been times when you doubted you would ever find happiness and peace of mind again. All the more reason to rejoice now.

Falling in love at any age can be quite a challenge. In retrospect, our first puppy love may have been too straightforward, although we probably didn't think so at the time. We waited with a beating heart for the phone to ring and, like most adolescents, mooned around when love went wrong. Then, after a while, the person whom we hoped would be 'the one' came along. We are blessed if this actually happens, but unfortunately for many men and women the union turns out not to be the right one. So, a second chance of happiness should be grasped with both hands.

Who knows what really makes us fall in love. Some people answer immediately: 'I loved her smile the first time I saw her' or 'I heard his voice on the phone, and I knew!' Other men and women talk of it taking time to get to know someone, and holding back on giving their heart until they are certain. Yet others have confided in me that they considered it was the time in their life to get married, and looked around for a suitable person.

If only we could have the foresight to enable us to see

which relationships will fail and which will stand the test of time! There is a saying, 'When poverty comes in the door love flies out of the window', but today it is more likely to be another person met at a party or in the office who causes the end of a marriage. But who knows if this is the real reason; it seems to me that somewhere in the partnership there already has to be a crack for that other person to find a way in.

There are many disillusioned men and women who believe that it is almost impossible to fall in love again, and this is especially so when they have been on the receiving end of betrayal, while others have the ability to move from one person to another with amazing speed. The key is to devote time to understanding, if you can, just what went wrong with the earlier relationship. Maybe even to reconcile yourself to accepting part of the blame. The more you can comprehend why an earlier partnership has not lasted, the more chance there is of true and enduring happiness second time around.

You will know of some couples whose relationship mystifies you when you try to understand the reason for their devoted love for each other. Questions such as 'What does he see in her?' or 'Why is she marrying him?' can never be answered from the outside. In fact, even the couple themselves may not be able to provide a satisfactory explanation. The truth is that some people just 'click' and it is a wonderful feeling when that happens. Let's call it falling in love.

Just the thought of marrying a second time may cause some people to freeze, often with fear. And it is sad, but true, that this fear and the anxiety it generates can result in a hesitation to accept a promise to love once more. But once that hurdle is overcome, then the glorious task of planning a second wedding day can begin.

Your wedding day

I have emphasised earlier in this book that if it is a first wedding for one of the bridal couple, it is all important that there should be no hint of it being second best in any way. This can't be repeated too often. If you have been married before, take immense trouble to reassure your new partner that this is going to be the best wedding day ever, and very special for both of you.

And make it happen. As we heard earlier, you may have to deal with some 'negative nellies' along the way, but disregard them. There are always people who are happy to pour cold water on other people's plans, so ignore them. And don't waste your energy trying to persuade anyone out of the mind-set that claims that 'just anything will do' for a second wedding. It won't. Don't accept for one moment that a second wedding *must* be a quiet affair. It doesn't have to be.

You should be as picky and selective as you need to be in planning the wedding ceremony and reception you both want. I have discussed ideas about alternative kinds of wedding services and receptions, and you should talk over together just what you want. It goes without saying that making the decision to marry is a very serious matter, but when you actually start to plan your second wedding, you should relax and thoroughly enjoy doing so. If you manage this, it will shine through on the actual day.

The major recent change for anyone wanting to remarry in the Church of England is the decision made by the General Synod to lift its ban on marrying divorcees where a former spouse is still living. It is still left entirely to individual clergy to decide whether or not to conduct a wedding, and they may evoke a 'conscience clause' if they disagree with this ruling. But the way is now clear. So, if it is a C of E wedding that you want, then you may have to search around, but couples are no longer bound to the parish where they live, and are free to try another church if the local priest refuses their request.

Couples are often distraught to find that one or other set of parents are troubled by plans made, and are even prejudiced about their child marrying a divorcee. But at the end of the day the prospective bride and groom must do what feels right for them. You may want to opt for a humanist wedding or a civil ceremony this time; and if you come up against opposition, you must stand firm. Often easier said than done I know, but remember, it is *your* wedding and you are both old enough to know what you want. And most likely you will be paying too.

You may be troubled knowing that the second marriages which do not survive are usually those where there are children from a previous relationship. Don't let your marriage break up for this reason. Be extra vigilant in foreseeing difficulties. Accept that it is hard for a parent to negotiate between an ex, a new spouse, and kids. See it the other way round, too, and appreciate how hard it is to be the 'new' person in a family which already exists. And, of course, you must always give special care to the children who are involved.

New beginnings

Once you have made the decision to marry, don't get so embroiled in all the preparations that you forget to have a good time. If you need help, look around for willing friends and relations. Just ask! You will be amazed to discover that people do like to be involved. You don't have to organise everything on your own. Give yourself plenty of time for the dozens of things which all brides and grooms have to do. Don't get into a fret – savour the moment.

You should keep in mind at all times what this wedding is about. You and your love have decided to show the world that you are a couple. That you love each other and want to spend the rest of your lives together. That is a many-splendoured thing, and something to hold on to through thick and thin.

Fortunately, this time you are not completely hide-bound by traditions; for a second wedding you have more leeway. So take advantage of this. Some people worry about whether friends who were at a first wedding should be invited to witness a second wedding, especially if they are still in touch with an ex-spouse. Should ex-in-laws be invited? And, oh dear, what about an ex-lover? Take a deep breath, and do just what you feel is the right thing for you. This too goes for gifts, what to wear, what to say ... and where to say it.

A wedding is a very personal affair, and this second wedding day should reflect back to the world the joy and hope you have for the future together. Even if you both decide you want a quiet wedding, let the bells ring out in your heart. A wedding day should be the happiest of days, so hold tight to the hand of your love, and face together whatever life may throw at you in the coming years. You know you are prepared. Hopefully, the sun will shine on your wedding day, and on your life together.

If only we'd known ...

'We have both been married before, and widowed. We are planning the most wonderful wedding; really dressed up, bells ringing, horse and carriage – the lot. People think we are mad, but that is what we want. We have both had so much grief in the past. I hope people will be happy for us on the day.'

11

Frequently asked questions

'To be, or not to be: that is the question.'
WILLIAM SHAKESPEARE, *Hamlet*

A second chance

Q. *Please send me details of all the information you have about a second wedding. What is appropriate?*

A. A rather terse e-mail like this makes it difficult to know just what is being asked. I need a few more details, especially about the areas where there is most concern.

Q. *We have lived together for eleven years. We have four kids. Now we think it would be nice to get married. Do you think people will laugh at us? What will the children think?*

A. It is great that you have decided to marry. Why ever not? Don't bother for a moment about 'what other people will think'. You both feel that this is the time to make your total commitment to each other in public. As it will be a real 'family wedding', I am sure the children will want to be involved, and there are many ways for them to contribute to the day.

Q. *My son is getting remarried. He has two children and his ex-wife has custody. I love my son and want to help this new relationship work, but he does not want me to have anything to do with his ex-wife whom I love very much. I want to visit my grandchildren in their mother's home, but this has made my son's future wife very unhappy. What should we do?*

A. Grandparents often suffer dreadfully from the fallout from a divorce. I can understand you want to support your son's new marriage, but don't jeopardise your relationship with your grandchildren. Quite likely after the wedding your son's new wife will feel more secure and so will hopefully not be so distressed about you seeing her husband's ex-wife.

Getting married again

Q. *I am getting married again in six months. We have both been married before. How do we tell our exes? My daughter has asked me to wait until after the holidays because 'It will break Dad's heart'. I am at my wits' end.*

A. I believe that ex-partners should be told as soon as possible. No sense in waiting, because there is an outside chance that an ex-spouse might hear of the news through the grapevine. And that is not a good idea. See 'Telling an ex' page 20.

Q. *Please advise: I was divorced last year, and now plan to marry at Christmas. Do I need to tell my ex-wife? She will probably hear from friends anyway.*

A. I do think that the 'right' thing to do is to tell your former wife yourself, before the news is heard on the grapevine. Even if your ex is now also married, learning about your wedding from a third party in a casual way can be very hard. So let your ex know as soon as possible.

Q. *I am at my wits' end. My future in-laws say that because my intended has been married before it is 'rude' if I send out invitations to his family members, and 'rude' to let his family members know where I have registered for gifts.*

A. It seems as if your future in-laws have got a real problem with the wedding. As they are picking on different aspects of your planning, perhaps your groom-to-be should clear the air with his parents.

Children and a second wedding

Q. *I am about to ask my girlfriend to marry me. She is a mother of three children – aged between nine and fifteen. They may have some idea of what is in the wind, but should we make a thing out of telling them? I am all for having a family party with both our parents, and telling them all in one go. Please tell me if this is OK?*

A. The children should be the first to be told, and it is best if this is done in private. They may have all kinds of different reactions, and questions to ask. So do this first, so that hopefully you will have a united family when you tell the news to your parents. See 'Children must be kept in the picture', page 36.

Q. *Any help would be appreciated. My divorce is not yet final, yet I plan to marry as soon as possible. My son of fifteen blames my new partner for the break-up (not altogether true). How can I get our old easy relationship back? He says he wants to live with his dad.*

A. At fifteen, I can understand your son may well have ideas of his own. After all, his world has been turned upside down, and it probably makes him feel better to have a 'say' as to where he will live. Don't rush it, and hope that at least he will come often and visit with you.

Q. *My dad is about to marry a woman with three children. I hate them and her, and they hate me. They keep telling me that as I am not of their blood we will not be family. My mum died two years ago. I feel so lonely. Help me!*

A. Is there anyone you can talk to? An auntie, grandparent or teacher? Try to tell your father too about feeling sad. Don't start off by saying 'they are being mean to me', but tell him that you are not happy and ask for his help. Let me know what happens.

Q. *My mother remarried last year and I was her bridesmaid. Now my dad is getting married but I do not want to be a bridesmaid this time. How can I tell him? I think it will make him angry. I haven't told anybody. I am fourteen.*

A. I think your mother should be able to help you out here. If it is difficult for you, perhaps she could explain to your father how you are feeling, and then you could talk to him about other ways you can be involved with his wedding day. Do write back and tell me what you think of this idea.

Planning the wedding

Q. *Our wedding – a second for us both – is planned for the autumn. Does it have to be a quiet affair?*

A. No, it does not. And one of the reasons I had for writing this book was to banish for ever the idea that a second wedding has to be an unceremonious or simple affair. Where there has been pain in the past, either through the death of a spouse or a divorce, most family and friends are delighted that happiness has been found again, and will be thrilled to dance at your wedding.

Q. *How can I get my husband-to-be more interested in our wedding plans? He has been married before – I haven't.*

A. Behind this question is the anxiety that this wedding is to be 'second best' for your fiancé? Some men can throw themselves into the detailed planning of a wedding, while others don't want to be involved and are content just to turn up at the right time! You should try to enjoy the wonderful joyous side of planning the wedding you want yourself. Think what a pleasant surprise the day is going to be for him.

Q. *We really do want a quiet wedding. Is it OK to slip off, and not to tell people? It is a second wedding for both of us, and neither of us have children.*

A. Yes, why ever not? Do just what pleases you and don't give a thought to 'what people will think'. You might have a party later, but only if you want to.

Q. *People say I am foolish to marry a man who is fifteen years*

228

older than I am. They say I will live to regret it, and it won't last. Are they right?

A. There are no guarantees about a marriage lasting, and the high rates of numbers of couples who divorce show that! If you love each other, go for it. You will always find people only too happy to pour cold water on lovers' plans.

Q. *My sister is getting married for the second time. Is it OK for me to organise a shower for her? I did it two years ago at the time of her first wedding.*

A. While many encore brides do like to have a shower, it is best to be guided by how a particular bride feels about this. In this case it may seem a little soon – especially if most of the guests will be the same as for the earlier shower!

Q. *Should my father pay for my second wedding? We think he should.*

A. When it is a second marriage most couples pay for their own wedding. Of course, there is nothing to stop parents contributing if they are able, or want to. But I don't feel you should expect a dad to pay up twice!

Q. *My dear partner and I are both pensioners. Do you think we are too old to have a wedding? What will people think?*

A. I think those who know you and love you will be only too delighted to share in the celebration of your wedding. Who said love and romance is only for the young?

Q. *It is a second marriage for us both, and we are spreading* *the news of our wedding by word of mouth. So far so good, but how can I make sure friends give us wedding gifts we want, and desperately need?*

A. Many second-wedding brides hesitate to register for gifts, and, especially as you have decided on an informal approach, the best way is by word of mouth. Do you have a close friend who could pass on details of what you are hoping for?

Q. *Do weddings have to cost the earth? This is a second one for us both, and we don't have much cash.*

A. No, they do not. Throughout this book there are suggestions for how to cut back on costs. Remember that the day is about your marriage, not about how much you spend on clothes and flowers. It is perfectly possible to have a lovely wedding day without breaking the bank. Celebrate with a picnic, or drinks and snacks with a small group of loving friends and family at home. If they know about your situation, they may all chip in, and why not? Ask a friend to take some photographs though, as these become treasures as the years go by.

Q. *Is there a good or bad time of the year to have a wedding? Last time I was married in December, in a blizzard.*

A. One of the benefits of getting married in the summer is that flowers are less expensive, and it is possible to take a chance and hold a reception out of doors – in a garden or park. Most couples try to avoid getting married around any public holidays, as friends may have plans to be out of town. One second-time bride went for the thirteenth of the month 'as this time it must be lucky!'

Where shall we marry?

Q. *How do I go about organising a service of blessing after my civil wedding? It will be my second wedding.*

A. The best way is to go to someone you would like to officiate at the blessing ceremony and *ask*. With more and more marriages taking place in register offices, having a service of blessing later in the day is becoming more popular and easier to arrange.

Q. *My fiancé lived in Scotland and told me he was 'married by habit and repute', yet is free for us to marry. Please explain*

A. 'Married by habit and repute' is a Scottish legal term for a common law marriage. All will depend upon whether he had his marriage recognised by the Court of Sessions.

Q. *I am a lesbian in the middle of a divorce. I would dearly love to marry my new partner. Is it possible in this day and age to do this?*

A. Affirmation or commitment ceremonies are becoming more popular for gay couples who want to be seen to be making a vow in public. See section on 'Gay and lesbian weddings' page 102.

Q. *Where can we get married that is really different? We have both been married before and I want to find a 'first'.*

A. A large department store in London has just been licensed to conduct civil marriages. Selfridges can arrange a marriage in the store, and they say they offer

'A truly modern celebration service'. Guests are able to give gifts in the form of a 'wedding account' which will be redeemed by the couple after their wedding day.

The reception

Q. *We want to marry abroad. Can we just fly off somewhere and marry?*

A. No, it is not as simple or romantic as this. You will be well advised to look at the section on 'Destination weddings' in this book where some of the formalities are listed.

Q. *I want help with ideas about a wedding which is different. Where shall I look?*

A. Read the sections in this book on 'Destination weddings' and 'Theme weddings'. Also, a good place to start is on the Internet. Donna, who is webhost to www.gettingremarried.com, said to me that she is dedicating her site 'to the encore bridal couple and their families'. She provides wedding vow suggestions, stepfamily, legal and religious information, a message board, and more. Another good starting point where you can post a message to other brides is www.weddingguide.co.uk. Also, try www.confetti.co.uk and www.topweddingsites.com for a full list of wedding sites on the Internet.

Q. *Is it true that you can get married without a residential requirement in Scotland? And I have been told that a* *religious ceremony can take place at any location. Is this right?*

A. Yes, it is correct that in Scotland you may marry without residential requirements. But formalities still have to be gone through in good time prior to the wedding. A marriage notice must be displayed at least fourteen days before the wedding. Then, if there have been no objections, a licence to marry is issued. (See the paragraph on Gretna Green on page 126.) And, yes, a religious ceremony can take place anywhere in Scotland, providing an authorised minister is in agreement.

Second wedding dilemmas

Q. *Who shall we have on the top table in place of the father of the bride who died recently?*

A. The problem was solved by a favourite uncle who was delighted to step in at the last moment and play his part with tact and sensitivity.

Q. *I want to wear a white dress although this is my second wedding. Is that OK?*

A. For a bride to wear white at a wedding is a comparatively recent tradition anyway, so why shouldn't you do so at a second wedding? However, second wedding tradition does decree that a long veil and train should be left to the first-time bride.

Q. *I want my little girl to be my flower-girl, but my mother says that it is tacky and 'not done'.*

A. I think that this is a lovely way for a mother to include her daughter at her second wedding. Couples who are remarrying are less bound by wedding traditions, so there is no reason why you should not go for it. Remember it is your wedding, not your mother's!

Q. *My sister was my bridesmaid at my first wedding. I am remarrying in September. Can she wear the same dress on this occasion?*

A. I like to think of a second wedding as a new beginning, and I think it would be a pity for your sister to wear something which would remind you all of your first wedding. If the cost of a new bridesmaid's dress is worrying you, have a look at the local charity shops which usually have the most wonderful bargains.

Q. *I am marrying a man who has been married before. I want him to dress with style this time. We are having a formal wedding. Any suggestions?*

A. If he is willing, why not a fancy waistcoat in keeping with your colour scheme? You can have fun browsing together through the website www.pocketwatchwaistcoats.co.uk.

Q. *I have been asked by a friend to give her away for her second marriage and her fiancé's first. What are my obligations, financial and other? I have NEVER done this before, even for a first-time marriage. Please help!*

A. The thing is that this is a tremendous honour. And you should enjoy every moment of it. I can't see that you have any financial obligations. You are there to accompany the bride to the side of her husband-to-be.

It doesn't depend upon where they are marrying, or if it is a second wedding for the bride, so just relax and enjoy this privilege.

Q. *It is my second wedding and my fiancé's third wedding. We want it to be a small and intimate ceremony, but will have a big reception within a month and show the video to everyone. We are also going to request donations to charities. I want it to be different. Any other ideas?*

A. You seem to have good ideas yourself for an original wedding. In my book there are suggestions for making weddings unique. Have you thought of a very different style of wedding cake? See page 214.

Children and remarriage

Q. *I am only twenty-two. Do I really have to have my future husband's adolescent children at the wedding? I am afraid they will spoil it.*

A. This young bride – and there are many of them – has not really taken on board just how much her life will be affected by these children. Because with so many second weddings there *are* children to consider, I have in this book spelt out the importance for all brides and grooms to consider the situation quite carefully if they are marrying someone who is a parent.

Q. *I am marrying a woman with two young children. I have a fourteen-year-old son who lives with me. Any tips for harmony?*

A. I think this dad is halfway there already. By asking this question he signals that he doesn't expect things to happen by magic. The formula for success is to take things slowly, go easy on handing out discipline to your partner's children, and accept that it will take time to settle into the new family.

Q. *Have you ever heard of kids on a honeymoon? My future husband wants his two children to come to the wedding, and then on the honeymoon. I am distraught. I have not been married before. What is the right thing to do?*

A. I think even the most unromantic of us would think it hard for this new bride to set off on her honeymoon with children if she does not wish to do so. Many couples do just that, and consider that after a 'family' wedding, there should be a 'family' holiday. However, as this bride is distraught, there needs to be some serious discussion between this couple right *now*! Surely a compromise can be found. See section 'How many on the honeymoon?', page 184.

Q. *My soon-to-be-wife and I have been living together for two years. Her kids, who all live with us, still treat me like a stranger. Will things get better after the wedding?*

A. There are no guarantees, but after the wedding the children will know you are here to stay, and they may begin to warm towards you. Don't believe that overnight you will become 'super stepdad' in their eyes. You can only go at their pace, and it will take time.

Q. *I have a new twelve-year-old stepdaughter whom I'm*

having a very hard time with. She does not show me any
respect. I get very upset and angry with her when she treats
me badly. Her mom and I are not getting along because
of the way I am handling things with her daughter. Please
give me some advice.

A. It is hardly ever easy to be a step-parent, but it is not easy
to be a twelve-year-old stepdaughter either. The painful
thing to accept is that love and respect of a parent is often
a given, whereas a step-parent has to earn it.

Q. *Help! My second marriage is in trouble. I want to go for*
custody of my son because his stepfather is verbally and
physically abusive to him. My wife feels that it would be a
burden for her to take care of him. She does not want him
here on a permanent basis. I think our marriage will end
if I get custody. I am so torn since I am going to lose
something, either my wife or my kid.

A. This must be one of the hardest situations for a parent
to face. I can understand your first loyalty is to your
child, and I suggest some marital counselling before the
relationship between you and your second wife
deteriorates further.

Q. *I am shortly marrying a man who has been divorced and*
who has a three-year-old little girl. I do worry that he still
wants to do things with his daughter and his ex-wife every
weekend. I think this is odd. What do you think? It took a
lot of courage to write to you.

A. I wonder if you have talked to your fiancé about your
worries? His daughter is still very little and may be
reluctant to leave her mother. However, is there any

way that as the wedding is approaching you could be included in some of the outings with dad and his daughter?

Q. *I have been a stepmother of four children for a year now. I have worked hard at being the best bonus mum I can be. All has been well until their mother came out of drug rehab and now she is involved with the children again they have developed an 'attitude' towards me. What do I do?*

A. The children probably do feel torn between you, as their bonus mother, and their own mother. I wonder if you know what she says to them? It must be hard for them that they now have to divide their lives between two homes. Give time for the dust to settle a bit.

Wedding traditions

Q. *It is a second wedding for my close friend. Do I have to give a super-duper present as I did last time?*

A. A very frequent question from friends and family who may have been very generous for a first wedding. Remember, there are many ways to select a gift. Something chosen with care which does not have to cost the earth will often mean a lot more to the couple than just another item ticked off their wedding list.

Q. *My mother died a month ago. We are going ahead with the wedding on Saturday – but how can we mark her absence?*

A. If you are having a religious service, ask the minister to include a prayer about your mother. One bride in a similar situation told me that she laid her bouquet on the chair where her mother would have sat at the service. Another couple lit a candle at the beginning of the service in memory of their parents. Yet another bride and groom said that between the service and the reception the couple went to the cemetery and laid a bouquet on the grave of a recently deceased parent.

Q. *I have been invited to a Hindu wedding. Is there anything I should know about its significance?*

A. A Hindu marriage is seen as a life-long commitment – a sacrament, not a contract. For more information about this ceremony see www.vivaaha.org.

Q. *This time I want to henna my hands for my wedding. Where can I buy stencils?*

A. Visit www.artemisimports.com/henna.htm – they supply henna kits and information.

Q. *I don't want to cut a traditional, white, tiered wedding cake for a second time. What do you suggest?*

A. You can easily go to town with different ideas, but if you want a designer cake made to specific requirements I am told you have to place your order nine to twelve months in advance. See the section on 'Wedding cakes' (page 214) for some alternative suggestions.

About my website

familyonwards.com
the jill curtis helpsite for parents and grandparents

My website www.familyonwards.com began four years ago as an Internet help and support site for parents, children and grandparents of divorce. Since then it has expanded to cover many other topics concerned with parenting and family issues.

Two of the most frequently accessed pages on the site are 'Second wedding ... second chance?' and 'Here comes the bride ... again!' which made me realise how many men and women are looking for suggestions and advice about a marriage where one or both have been married previously.

There are over 150 other articles on family issues on the site, a regular 'article of the month', and other new pieces are frequently added. There is an ever-growing section of book reviews on topics such as domestic violence, marriage, parenting, children with special needs, grandparenting, health, women's issues, gay family issues and more. There are also links to other carefully selected helpful Internet sites.

I hope you will visit the site and contact me on www.familyonwards.com.